THE
(ALMOST)
ZERO
WASTE
GUIDE

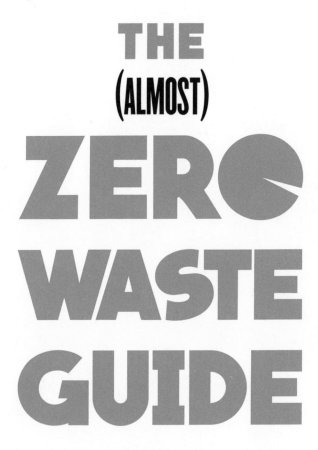

THE (ALMOST) ZERO WASTE GUIDE

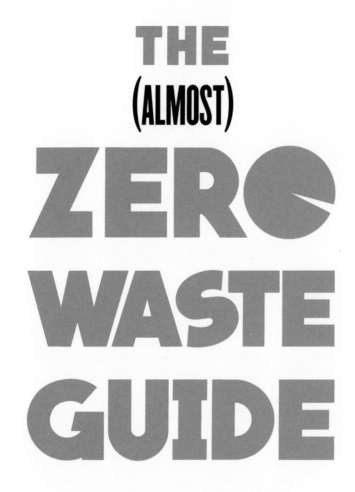

100+ TIPS FOR REDUCING YOUR WASTE WITHOUT CHANGING YOUR LIFE

MELANIE MANNARINO

TILLER PRESS

New York   London   Toronto   Sydney   New Delhi

An Imprint of Simon & Schuster, Inc.
1230 Avenue of the Americas
New York, NY 10020

First Tiller Press trade paperback edition January 2021

TILLER PRESS and colophon are trademarks of
Simon & Schuster, Inc.

For information about special discounts for bulk purchases,
please contact Simon & Schuster Special Sales at 1-866-506-1949
or business@simonandschuster.com.

The Simon & Schuster Speakers Bureau can bring authors to
your live event. For more information or to book an event,
contact the Simon & Schuster Speakers Bureau at 1-866-248-3049
or visit our website at www.simonspeakers.com.

Interior design by Jennifer Chung

Manufactured in the United States of America

1 3 5 7 9 10 8 6 4 2

Library of Congress Cataloging-in-Publication Data
Names: Mannarino, Melanie, author.
Title: The (almost) zero waste guide : 100+ tips for reducing your
waste without changing your life / Melanie Mannarino.
Description: New York : Tiller Press, 2020. | Includes index.
Identifiers: LCCN 2019056186 (print) | LCCN 2019056187 (ebook) |
ISBN 9781982142230 (paperback) | ISBN 9781982142247 (ebook)
Subjects: LCSH: Sustainable living. | Waste minimization. | Recycling
(Waste, etc.) | Household supplies. | Green products. | Environmental
responsibility.
Classification: LCC GF196 .M36 2020 (print) |
LCC GF196 (ebook) | DDC 640.28/6—dc23
LC record available at https://lccn.loc.gov/2019056186
LC ebook record available at https://lccn.loc.gov/2019056187

ISBN 978-1-9821-4223-0
ISBN 978-1-9821-4224-7 (ebook)

Contents

Introduction

There are people on this planet—in different countries and cities and towns—whose discarded trash for a year fits tidily in one glass Mason jar. These environmental heroes have mastered the art of living as close to zero waste as possible.

I am not one of those people.

True zero waste, of course, is when everything humans produce or use either gets consumed in its entirety (like, say, a sandwich), reused (the ceramic plate the sandwich is on), recycled (the plastic bag the bread came in), or composted back into the land to fertilize the soil (the core from the lettuce leaf on the sandwich). Nothing gets incinerated or sent to a landfill or ends up in the ocean or air to pollute the environment.

In this way, we leave no indelible mark (or, honestly, scar) on our planet. No landfills teeming with discarded armchairs, dirty diapers, and food scraps buried so deep that they can't decompose naturally and instead do so without air, creating methane that contributes to climate change. No industrial-size incinerators burning materials we no longer need and darkening our skies with smoke and chemicals. No plastics—from grocery bags to facial scrub microbeads—in our water supply, consumed by ocean life that we in turn eat for dinner.

It's enough to make you want to slam the brakes on your current consumer lifestyle and grab that Mason jar, right? Except for most of us—once we start looking around our home, our workplace, and even our car—it's incredibly easy to get overwhelmed by the sheer amount of waste being generated every minute of every day. While writing this paragraph, I used a tissue and threw it in the wastebasket, wrote a to-do list on a sticky note, took a sip from a plastic drinking cup, and considered making shrimp for dinner—shrimp that's currently sitting in a sealed plastic bag in my freezer. I'm typing on a computer that will one day wear out, checking a phone that will become obsolete, and being shielded from the sun by lowered honeycomb window shades that will eventually break and need to be replaced.

But you know what? I have a rainwater collection system in my backyard, I buy secondhand furniture, and on countless occasions I've said to my little boy, "Why would we buy those packaged cookies/Halloween costumes/holiday decorations when we could make them ourselves?" In fact, many of the ideas in this book come straight from my own life.

To be honest, there's no way I could ever take myself and my family from typical modern consumer household to zero-waste household in one giant lifestyle makeover. It's a huge commitment in terms of time, budget, resources, and behavioral change, and it's just not feasible at the moment. What *is* feasible, though, is incorporating more and more ways to reduce our household and personal waste, one lifestyle tweak at a time. Consider it (almost) zero waste.

You don't have to adopt an all-or-nothing zero-waste lifestyle to live more sustainably and be more environmentally friendly. Every single step you take to reduce the waste you create—from car exhaust to plastic wrap—lessens your overall impact on your community and the planet. Actively striving toward zero waste is an accomplishment itself. The journey is the thing—it's something to *do* in a world where, environmentally speaking, there's a lot of bad news. Humans have driven greenhouse-gas emissions to unprecedented levels, which contributes to climate change. Globally, we dump 2.01 billion tons of waste in landfills[1] each year. One quarter of the world's population experiences extreme levels of water stress[2]—meaning they could be one short dry spell away from crisis. Here in the United

States, water scarcity can happen for many different reasons, from not being able to pay one's bills to local water supplies literally drying up.[3]

So if you're feeling inspired to change your habits in order to reduce your consumption of natural resources, or to simply reduce the waste you produce, I'm here to tell you that you can easily do it. If shutting off the faucet while you brush your teeth can help save a little water now so that we have more later in case we really need it, do it. If using the broken shards of your grandmother's serving platter to make a cool mosaic not only keeps them out of the landfill but also preserves a visual memory, do it. Every time one of us refuses a straw or a handful of plastic utensils, we're reducing the amount of single-use plastics needing disposal in one way or another.

A Zero-Waste Cheat Sheet

Every little thing we do makes a difference, and in this book I've outlined more than one hundred changes you can make in your daily life that will reduce your environmental impact in terms of pollution, energy usage, food waste, and more. These actionable tips address unseen waste—the stuff we don't "throw out," like vehicle emissions, electrical energy, and water—as well as the tangible waste we do see, like worn-out running shoes and used kitty litter. Try one at a time, or start all of them tomorrow—the choice is yours. Only you know which options make sense for you.

In fact, I'm willing to bet that right this minute you could look around your home or your office and identify a handful of simple changes you could make. We know what we're doing "wrong"; it's a matter of identifying a way to do it "right" that fits with your individual lifestyle.

As you read the (almost) zero-waste strategies and ideas in this book, you'll start to notice a pattern: each one fits neatly into one of the central behaviors of a zero-waste lifestyle. Darby Hoover, senior resource specialist for the Natural Resources Defense Council (NRDC), sums it up succinctly: "Reduce, reuse, recycle." That mandate isn't new—it dates back to the 1970s. But it's catchy and easy to remember, and it tells us all we need to know to start working toward zero waste.

- Think about where you can **reduce** the
  materials or energy you use to get through

your day. Bring your own travel mug to the coffee shop instead of accepting a plastic-lined paper to-go cup (they're generally not recyclable, BTW).

- **Reuse** materials wherever you can. Do you need to buy a black-tie outfit for that wedding, or can you rent one or borrow from a friend?

- **Recycle** everything you possibly can to drive down the amount of waste that goes to the landfill, doomed to decompose anaerobically (without oxygen), releasing methane into our air and accelerating climate change even further.

The Myth of Throwing Things Away

We're constantly throwing things away. The half-eaten office birthday cake? It gets thrown away at the end of the day. Candy wrappers and chip bags? They get thrown away. A pair of holey socks? Thrown away.

We don't always think about what happens next, do we? We toss an item into the trash bin, and from there it goes to the garbage collectors, who bring it to the dump. The cake, the chip bags, and the socks are now out of our minds and our lives.

Except they're not really out of our lives. Waste is overrunning our planet, says Hoover. "The idea that there is an 'away'—our world isn't big enough for that anymore," she says. "There is no 'away.'" And yet we continue to think there is. "Recycling has become the 'good away,' unlike the landfill, which is 'bad away,'" she says. "But this can't be our sole solution." At a certain point, that landfill is going to be so large that it will literally be in our own backyard.

We need to reframe the idea of throwing things "away." Consider the birthday cake: Could it have been offered to colleagues in another department shortly after the birthday celebration was over? If the cake had been fully eaten, and the knife and plate used to serve it washed and put back in the staff kitchen, there would be nothing to throw away at all. Would that (clean) holey sock make a good mitt for dusting baseboards and other surfaces? Eliminating the chip bag might take a little more effort—slice and deep-fry your own potatoes, perhaps?—but at the very least, you can make sure to buy the family-size bag and eat a serving at a time, rather than laying in a supply of single-serving bags (which make for more waste per serving).

As you start to set aside your vegetable peels to add to a garden compost heap, reduce your reliance on single-use plastics like zip-top bags and flatware, and consider whether a damaged item could be fixed rather than tossed, you'll find that you're generating less waste in general—and relying less on both the "good away" (recycling) and the "bad away" (landfill). Zero waste? Maybe not yet. But almost.

Things You Can't Unsee

Since writing this book, I can never look at my shampoo bottle the same way again.

Oh, I've been recycling the bright-pink plastic tube since recycling was a thing. And I felt pretty good about getting every last drop out before chucking it into the bin. I use cuticle scissors to cut it open at the end, swiping my finger around the half-tube to get another few days' worth of product. (And then I give it a full rinse before recycling.) Not only that, I don't even shampoo every day—more like every other. *I'm so efficient in my consumption,* I tell myself. *I'm a conscious consumer!*

Then I learned that only 14 percent of all the plastic ever produced has been recycled, and that even what seems like a small amount of contamination in a batch of recycling—say, peanut butter residue in a jar, or an unrinsed bottle of tomato juice—could get the entire batch rejected and sent to the landfill anyway. My efforts matter, but are they really having the impact I want?

So I'm faced with a choice: either keep doing what I'm doing, or try a different strategy. I could shop around for a larger-size bottle of my shampoo, on the principle that smaller packaging results in more waste overall for an equal amount of product. I could find a bulk beauty supply store near me that allows me to bring in my own reusable container and fill it with their shampoo. Or I could try bar shampoo and completely eliminate the need for plastic packaging or even a reusable bottle.

Once you open your eyes to the waste all around you, you'll face a lot of choices like mine—and what you decide is ultimately up to you. You might think twice before tossing kale stems into the kitchen waste bin or throwing last summer's worn-out flip-flops into the garbage can at the curb. There are tips in this book for all of those moments—different paths you can take, each leading you toward an (almost) zero-waste life-style. You might make your own trade-offs, and you'll find certain tips easier to work into your life than others. But at every step, you'll be more thoughtful about how you navigate through your life.

Don't just rely on my permission, though. Darby Hoover of the NRDC offers her own take on things—and she's been working in the field for more than thirty years. "The world isn't going to end because you bought one bottle of water when you were thirsty," she says. "Understand where you *can* do stuff, and forgive yourself for everything else. Don't beat yourself up so much that you put your head in the sand." Doing even one thing is always better than doing nothing.

A Modern-Day Rock-Paper-Scissors

When you set out to make changes in your daily life, you might find yourself choosing the lesser of two evils.

Should you buy the ice cream in the cardboard carton or the plastic tub? Should you buy a leather jacket made from methane-producing, land-occupying cows, or a vegan one made from PVC (a plastic)? While doing research for this book, I found myself wondering whether there was a hard-and-fast hierarchy: is saving water more important than avoiding plastic, which is more important than wasting trees? (And if there was a hierarchy, how could I turn it into a cool graphic that we could all refer to daily?)

It turns out that there's no real hierarchy. Instead, says Hoover, we need to ask ourselves these questions: Could I do this with fewer resources (like water or electricity or fuel)? Does one item have less packaging than a similar one? Does it contain recycled content? Look to make better choices, and those will be the *right* choices.

And that brings me to this book itself. If you're reading it on a device, you won't need to figure out what to do with it once you're done. If you're reading a paper copy, please know that I tried to keep all the advice here as concise and specific as possible so that I didn't waste pages and pages made from precious wood pulp by babbling needlessly. In the spirit of zero waste, once you're done with this book, donate it to a library or a used bookshop, or share it with a friend. Encourage your friend to lend it to another friend once they're finished, and so on and so on. Not only will that keep this book out of the landfill or re-cycling center but it will also spread the message that every choice we make can bring us one step closer to living (almost) zero waste.

ONE

Eat and Cook (Almost) Zero Waste

There was a time, generations ago, when the majority of the country ate zero waste. When you raise your own animals, grow your own food, and prepare meals from scratch, you generate very little waste (especially if you compost the food scraps to fertilize your next crop). However, we live in modern times, and many of us buy a week's supply of food at a time, bringing home animal protein packed in plastic wrap and Styrofoam, cookies and crackers sealed in plastic bags within cardboard boxes, dairy in plastic containers, and fruits and vegetables bagged in plastic. What we don't eat, we often throw out once it's past its sell-by date, and what we don't buy in time, super-markets, restaurants, and other retail food stores must throw out or donate to charity (they're not legally allowed to give it away at the end of the day). According to the NRDC, 40 percent of food in the United States goes uneaten, and food waste is the largest component of the solid waste in landfills.[1]

So how do we get back to that more efficient way of eating—and still enjoy the convenience of everything from supermarket-prepared meals and fine dining to theme-park snacks and road-trip eats? There are big and small steps we can all take, every day, to reduce the amount of food- and food-related waste in this country. This list is a great starting point, but as you challenge yourself to tweak your lifestyle habits and embrace an (almost) zero-waste diet, you may find even more ways to scale back on what you toss, while enjoying every bite.

DITCH THE STRAW.

Plastic straws are an iconic example of the ubiquity of single-use plastics in modern living. One commonly cited stat (based on data from straw manufacturers) is that in the United States alone, five hundred million straws are used per day (which averages out to roughly 1.6 straws per person).[2] Unfortunately, some of those straws become litter when people don't discard them properly. Others make it into the recycling bin, but because straws are lightweight, they may not be properly sorted at the recycling plant and could end up as refuse. When plastic straws get into our oceans, they eventually break down into microplastics and are consumed by marine creatures like fish and seabirds—with often fatal results.[3]

For many of us, the answer is simple: use stainless steel, glass, silicone, or bamboo straws at home, and bring travel straws when on the go (give them a quick rinse after you're finished, and then clean them thoroughly once you're home). While some people with special needs or specific circumstances must use plastic straws specifically to drink effectively, the rest of us can do our part to reduce the amount of plastic straws used daily.

Which Reusable Straw Is Right for You?

STAINLESS STEEL: This fully recyclable metal is durable, nonbreakable, and dishwasher-safe.

It also gets supercold when you sip cold beverages, and equally hot when you're drinking warm liquids (whether that's a problem for you is a matter of personal preference). Stainless steel is also opaque, so if you want to *see* that your straw is truly clean, this isn't the material for you.

GLASS: Quality versions are made with borosilicate, an especially sturdy ingredient that's also used in Pyrex glassware. This makes them resistant to heat and cold; they won't crack in extreme temperatures. But they *can* crack or shatter if dropped, so clumsy people and children might want to choose another option. (On the plus side: you can easily see how clean your straw is after that peanut-butter-and-banana smoothie!)

BAMBOO: Sustainable bamboo makes an ideal straw in its natural state; no extensive manufacturing required. These straws are also biodegradable and compostable, so if you want to compost one after a single use, feel free. However, they do wear out (usually by starting to splinter), so they're not as durable as other options.

SILICONE: The big pro here is that you can bite on these straws the way you might on plastic straws without chipping a tooth. Additionally, these dishwasher-safe straws don't leach chemicals when subjected to extreme temperatures (as plastic can).

PAPER: While this alternative to plastic straws may not immediately threaten marine life the way plastic will, it's not really a zero-waste option. Once used, soiled paper straws are likely to go into regular garbage (rather than recycling), where they'll head to a landfill and decompose, releasing methane gas into the atmosphere.[4]

ORDER ONLY AS MUCH FOOD AS YOU CAN EAT.

It's a classic piece of advice from budget-travel experts: to cut down on dining-out costs, order an appetizer (or two) instead of an entree. But it's not just a money-saving tactic, it's also one that can reduce food waste. Anything you leave on your plate, of course, will go right into the trash once your server removes it from your table. And given that the average restaurant meal contains 1,205 calories—about half the recommended daily intake[5]—chances are you're definitely not cleaning your plate. Overall, the restaurant industry generates about 11.4 million tons of food waste annually.[6] Help reduce that by ordering only what you can eat in one sitting.

BRING YOUR OWN TO-GO CONTAINERS.

Not as hungry as you thought? Couldn't resist the entree special of the day? (Or, even more tempting, those buy-one, take-one-home meal deals some chain restaurants offer?) Not a problem: just make sure to tuck an earth-friendly to-go container into your bag before you leave home. Then, after your meal, depending on the fancy-factor of the restaurant, you can either gently push your leftovers from your plate into your container or ask the server to do it for you in the kitchen. A stainless steel container with a tight seal makes for a smart, durable option.

SKIP THE TAKEOUT.

Treat yourself—and the planet—right by skipping takeout or delivery meals. To-go food usually arrives in a plastic or paper bag (sometimes one nestled within the other), in one or more plastic, cardboard, or Styrofoam containers—sometimes divided by pieces of cardboard for stability—along with plastic utensils and paper napkins. Instead, make a meal at home or dine at the takeout joint, where you can bring your own utensils, cloth napkin, and to-go container for leftovers if you'd like.

BREW YOUR DARK ROAST AT HOME.

Whether you're a pour-over fanatic or more "cold brew or bust," making your own coffee drinks at home (and transporting them in your favorite reusable beverage holder) is the easiest way to get your fix, eliminate the waste that comes from to-go joe (paper cups, plastic lids, store receipts), and retain control over the coffee waste that comes from brewing in any setting. Compost slow-decomposing coffee grounds to add nitrogen and other nutrients to your mix, and possibly even attract more worms (which are essential for aeration, keeping your fertilizer-to-be extra healthy). Just don't get any DIY body scrub ideas: coffee grounds are notorious for clogging drains.

SWITCH TO LOOSE-LEAF TEA.

Many (but not all) tea manufacturers have switched from plastic tea bags to paper ones in recent years, but there is still concern over the glue used to seal each bag, which may not be biodegradable.[7] What that means for you: it will never fully decompose in a landfill or in your compost. To truly reduce waste, make the switch to loose-leaf teas. They often come in decorative, reusable tins (or you could always bring your own to your new favorite loose-leaf tea retailer), and in more varieties and blends than you'd find on a typical supermarket shelf. To make a cup, place the suggested serving of tea leaves in a stainless steel tea ball, drop into your hot water to steep, and enjoy!

Buy in bulk.

No, we're not talking about buying a huge box of single-serving snacks from the nearest warehouse club. You can actually find bulk bins of grain, beans, nuts, dried fruit, coffee, tea, flour, sugar, and even prepared foods like cereals and granolas at both larger supermarkets and smaller independent markets. Some co-ops and other indie markets even offer liquids like vinegar and oil in bulk, and some nut butters. Check a store's website or drop in before buying to see if they have any restrictions on customers bringing their own containers. Once you know the rules, bring your own cloth bags, glass jars, or other zero-waste-friendly containers and ask the salesperson to weigh (tare) your container before you add food to it so you don't get charged extra for the weight of your container. And make sure to label your jars so you remember what you've got once you bring it home—using a grease pencil or glass-marking pencil directly on the container will do the trick without creating more waste.

MAXIMIZE MEATS.

Like other groceries, meats (chicken, beef, fish—whatever) can often be purchased using your own container. Just ask at your local supermarket, butcher, or farm-stand vendor. In the kitchen, take tonight's dinner from a "single-use" meal to a repurposed one: save bones in the freezer until you have enough to simmer with water and aromatics to make your own stock. Likewise, shrimp and lobster shells—as well as the cooking liquid from steamed mussels and clams—make excellent seafood stock.

STEER CLEAR OF SINGLE-SERVING PACKAGES.

Yes, they offer built-in portion control—but with that convenience comes excess packaging, whether plastic containers or bags, metal wrappers, or additional cardboard. A better way to divvy up crackers and other snacks: buy the largest package available (after checking the bulk bins first), then portion everything into stainless steel containers, silicone zip-top bags, or small, reusable glass jars (like repurposed baby food jars, pickle jars, jam jars, or salsa jars).

WHEN IN DOUBT, CHOOSE GLASS OR METAL OVER PLASTIC.

Every once in a while, you may encounter a food or condiment you can't buy in bulk. When that happens, opt for the version that comes in a glass or metal container, rather than a plastic one. A glass jar, in particular, can be repurposed in dozens of different practical and decorative ways once emptied and cleaned. Here are just a few ideas:

- Desktop organizer (for pens, pencils, scissors, etc.)
- Vanity organizer (for nail files, makeup pencils, and brushes)
- Vase
- Drinking glass
- Salad dressing container
- Seashell display
- Mini terrarium
- Dried herb and spice containers
- Mini herb garden
- Sand art

STASH REUSABLE BAGS EVERYWHERE.

In your car. In your bicycle basket. In your tote bag, backpack, or briefcase. In your handbag. This ensures that you'll never have to accept a paper or plastic bag when you make a purchase from a grocery store or farmers' market. And when you use one (or more), as soon as you bring them into the house and unpack your items, immediately return the bags to where they came from. (Because a reusable bag can't help save the planet if it's tucked away in your coat closet.)

BUT DON'T GO OUT AND BUY NEW REUSABLE BAGS.

We think of thin plastic shopping bags as the height of environmental waste, but some research[8] has determined that the process used to manufacture reusable totes (cotton or otherwise) has a larger negative impact on water use, air pollution, climate change, and ozone depletion.[9] In fact, according to the Life Cycle Assessment Study of Grocery Carrier Bags conducted by the Ministry of Environment and Food of Denmark, an organic cotton tote would have to be reused 149 times to equal the climate change impact of a plastic bag. The practical takeaway? If you have plastic bags in your home, use them as often as possible before dropping them into a recycling bin (look for specific boxes at your grocery store, or check to see if there are central drop-off points at your town hall or public library). And if you have totes made of cotton or other textiles, use them again and again, too—just don't rush out and buy a new trove of eco-friendly bags, because you might be doing more harm than good.

How Clean Is That Reusable Bag?

BAGS—especially those used to tote produce, meats, and other groceries—get dirty. A reusable shopping bag study[10] conducted by Dr. Ryan Sinclair of Arizona's Loma Linda University found large amounts of bacteria present in nearly all bags, and *E. coli* in 12 percent of them. Worse, bags contaminated by meat juices for two hours and then left in a warm environment had ten times the amount of bacteria. Gross, yes—but the study also found that hand or machine washing reduced the bacteria in bags by more than 99.9 percent. For non-machine-washable bags, spritzing a food-safe antibacterial cleanser on the interior and thoroughly wiping with a cloth might

be enough. But for all others, frequent machine washing can keep your bags bacteria
free—and keep you from getting sick.

GROW YOUR OWN FOOD.

If you've got a sunny windowsill, you can grow herbs.
A balcony? Planter tomatoes. A patch in your yard?
Any fruit or vegetable you want (that happens to thrive
in your geographical location). The simplest way to
lessen your environmental footprint is to grow your
own food, right in your own backyard. The "farm"-
to-table distance couldn't be shorter, you control
everything from seeds to soil (so there's no chance
of carcinogenic fertilizers or insecticides being used),
and you'll naturally eat seasonally. What's more, you
can compost produce scraps and sometimes the plants
themselves (as long as they aren't diseased) at the end
of the season, then use that compost to nourish next
year's crop. The *Old Farmer's Almanac* lists ten of the
easiest vegetables to grow from seed:[11] beans, beets,
carrots, cucumbers, kale, lettuce, peas, pumpkins, rad-
ishes, and squash.

EAT WITH THE SEASONS.

The shorter the distance a fruit or vegetable travels
from the farm to your table, the smaller the environ-

mental impact it has. While that might mean that those of us in a four-season climate have to deny our blueberry cravings in the dead of winter, it will result in less fuel waste. One easy way to do this is to shop your farmers' market—everything there should be local and seasonal. If there are no year-round farmers' markets in your area, keep an eye out for labels indicating "local produce" at your supermarket. As more people become aware of the impact of buying a tomato that's traveled across at least one continent before purchase, stores are becoming increasingly transparent about where a fruit or vegetable was grown.

COOK WITH FRUIT AND VEGETABLE SCRAPS.

Did you know that radish tops, ramp tops (ramps are cousins of leeks and shallots), and beet greens all make delicious pesto? Carrot greens can be sautéed with garlic and oil like spinach or kale, or blended into a flavorful chimichurri sauce. You can also eat the leaves of turnips, broccoli, cauliflower, and brussels sprouts (just remove the tough ribs first)—like sweet potato leaves, they're good sautéed or added to soups. Another zero-waste soup tip: chopped lacinato (dinosaur) kale stems add tender-crunchy body and texture to bean and other soups. Other creative ways to eat the parts of fruits and vegetables we usually discard:

- Pickled watermelon rind: In a boiled brine of vinegar, sugar, and spices like cinnamon, ginger, allspice, and clove
- Vegetable broth: Save the ends of carrots, onions, celery, and other vegetables—and the stems of herbs like parsley—in the freezer till you have enough to make a flavorful broth
- Vanilla sugar: Add the scraped-out pod to a container of granulated sugar and store until fragrant
- Candied citrus peel: Bring to a boil, then simmer in a 1:1 sugar-water solution
- Fried potato peels: Deep-fry or air fry, then season with salt and your favorite spice mix
- Stir-fried broccoli stalk "coins": Peel thick stems before cooking and then compost the peels
- Corn cob chowder: Use corn cobs to make a flavorful corn stock with onion, celery, and other aromatics and then add puréed and whole kernels to the chowder toward the end

GIVE OTHER FOOD SCRAPS A SECOND LIFE.

Stale bread makes great bread crumbs (pulse in a food processor and then freeze until needed) or croutons (cube, toss with oil, garlic, and herbs, and then bake), as well as French toast, berry pudding, or savory strata. Hard cheese rinds like Parmesan and pecorino romano can be frozen and then thrown into your next batch of soup as the broth simmers for rich umami flavor.

MENU PLAN.

A little menu planning goes a long way in an (almost) zero-waste lifestyle. When you plot out your meals, you can then make detailed grocery lists and buy only what you need and know you will eat. Love leftovers? Plan to double your recipe and eat it for days. Hate leftovers? Adjust your recipe to make only the number of portions you need for one meal. Look at your calendar and map out what days you can cook and eat at home, how many others in your household will be eating the food, and how much time you have to prepare (a Tuesday night might not be the best time to make a vegetarian cassoulet from scratch). If you food shop only at the beginning of the week, plan to use your most perishable ingredients earlier in the week (think chicken, fish, and already-ripe vegetables) and save the hardier ones for week's end (beans and grains).

Why Meatless Monday Is a Thing

Meatless Monday might seem like a modern solution to reducing the amount of greenhouse-gas-producing meat we eat, but it actually got started during World War I as a way to reduce consumption, according to the Monday Campaigns, an organization that brought back the idea in 2003[12] as a means of improving the health of Americans (who now eat an average of seventy-five more pounds of meat per year than previous generations). Today, Meatless Monday is practiced around the world, not only for personal health reasons but also to reduce the environmental impact of meat-eating on the planet. According to a 2018 study,[13] while more than 80 percent of farmland is used for livestock, it results in just 18 percent of food calories and 37 percent of protein. What's more, livestock raised for beef contribute twelve times more greenhouse-gas emissions than dairy cows, which in turn produce twenty-six times more than peas. If you want to reduce waste in the form of greenhouse gases, cutting back your meat consumption is a smart step.

REUSE COOKING WATER.

Let your cooking water cool before storing it in the fridge for a second use. Save starchy pasta water to give extra body to puréed soups (like chowders and squash-, potato-, and cauliflower-based blends). Repurpose water used to boil vegetables as a base for homemade stocks. If the water is unsalted, you can even use it to water your herb, fruit and vegetable, or flower garden.

COMPOST WHATEVER FOOD SCRAPS ARE LEFT.

On first thought, it might seem unnecessary to compost your food scraps unless you have a garden that would benefit from the nutrient-rich fertilizer/soil conditioner it creates. After all, food decomposes, whether in a public landfill or your backyard compost heap, right? While that's all true on the surface, the truth is a lot, well, deeper. When food scraps go into your kitchen garbage bag and get hauled to the dump, they end up being buried deep within other piles of refuse and decomposing without oxygen. This oxygen-free decomposition produces methane gas, a greenhouse gas that contributes to climate change. In contrast, food scraps that are composted (by you or your community) have the opportunity to decompose in an oxygen-rich environment, so they break down without releasing methane.

Food scraps and yard waste (also compostable) currently make up 30 percent of landfill waste in the United States,[14] according to the EPA. Composting can help drive that percentage down and keep our air cleaner. Plus, it also gives you an amazing soil supplement you can use in your herb and vegetable garden or flower beds. Your food scraps get a second life and help new plants grow and flourish; it's an all-around win. It's also easy to get started: you need a small container for your kitchen, where you can stash food scraps as you cook and prep, as well as a large outdoor compost container, where the decomposition magic will happen.

Some people keep a small lidded canister or bin right on their countertops, where they can throw scraps throughout the day. You can buy a canister made for compost scraps (some come with a charcoal filter to reduce odors), or you can repurpose one of your own. To reduce the possibility of attracting fruit flies or other insects, take your compost out daily. Some composters find that storing scraps in the fridge or freezer also keeps bugs away.

To compost your scraps outdoors, you can buy a compost container or create your own using repurposed wooden fencing, pallets, a plastic garbage bin, or another container. (You don't even need a yard for this—if you've got room on a balcony, try it!) The essential ingredients for successful compost are carbon, nitrogen, moisture, and air. Layering in different compost materials can give you the proper mix of carbon and nitrogen, and keeping the soil damp and turning it frequently will help everything decompose properly. A few things cannot be composted, including pet waste, animal products (dairy or meat), and any yard clippings or plants treated with pesticides. Otherwise, here's the list of materials you can safely compost:

Nitrogen-rich Compostable Materials[15]

- Sawdust
- Wood chips
- Pine needles
- Dried leaves
- Straw
- Recycled paper and cardboard

- Dried grass
- Shredded paper
- Shredded newspaper
- Potting soil

Carbon-rich Compostable Materials

- Fruit and vegetable scraps
- Citrus rinds
- Coffee grounds and filters
- Non-greasy rice, pasta, bread, cereal
- Tea bags (make sure the bags are compostable; see page 7 for more details)
- Egg and nut shells
- Pits
- Cut or dried flowers
- Houseplants
- Soiled brown paper products

MAKE YOUR OWN BABY FOOD.

While you're cooking vegetables and other whole foods for the night or the week, why not purée a batch for the little one? Your pediatrician can give you a list of starter foods appropriate for your baby's age and stage. After that, shop your garden, your CSA box, or your local market for the best produce available, and then cook and purée it to the right consistency. Store it in freezer-safe canning jars or freeze individual portions in ice cube trays and use as needed.

Buy a seltzer maker.

If bubbles are your life, you have two options: keep buying the largest-size plastic or glass bottle of sparkling water you can find, or buy a seltzer maker so you can have bubbles on demand at all times, served from your own reusable bottle. To feel better about the purchase, consider the typical number of bottles of sparkling water you go through in a month, multiply that by twelve, and imagine those bottles lined up next to a seltzer machine. A machine will last you years, and the only materials you'll need to recycle are the CO_2 cartridges that give your beverage its fizz.

Know what the date on your food means.

"Sell by," "best by," "use by" . . . the terms and dates on groceries like dairy products, meats, and packaged foods can be confusing—and cause an estimated 20 percent of food waste in the home. Different manufacturers use different language to inform consumers that a product's nutrition, quality, and taste is promised until that date—but not after. What these dates do *not* mean is that the product will immediately spoil or become unsafe to eat once that date has come and gone. In fact, to clear up this confusion, the FDA is currently supporting the food industry as they work to streamline the language used across all products, so that in the future you might see only the words "Best if used by."[16]

How to Tell When Food's Gone Bad

The Foodkeeper app, developed by the USDA's Food Safety and Inspection Service, Cornell University, and the Food Marketing Institute, offers item-specific information on how long foods stay fresh in the refrigerator and the freezer, as well as the proper times and temperatures at which to cook them. You can download the app to your mobile phone or find it in your browser. Beyond that, your senses can tell you whether a certain food has taken a turn for the worse, sometimes more accurately than any date on the packaging.

IT SMELLS FUNNY. If your uncooked meat or fish has an odd or sulfuric odor, don't take a chance. Sour milk is another smell you don't want to ignore.

IT'S GROWING THINGS. Green mold on your shredded cheese or bread, an odd white substance on the top of your salsa . . . in many instances, bacteria can penetrate far beyond what you see.

THE TEXTURE HAS CHANGED. Separated, curdled-looking—or, worse, lumpy—dairy products indicate freshness has long past. Slimy deli meats or vegetables are another indication of food that's been kept for too long.

Two

Create an (Almost) Zero-Waste Home

Americans generate a lot of waste: 4.48 pounds per person per day,[1] according to the most recent EPA figures (from 2015). And while some of that is surely discarded on the go—at work, at school, while running errands—most of it is likely tossed at home (especially when you consider that "waste" includes anything we throw away after use, including old couches, broken dishes, used notebooks, worn area rugs, etc.).

Clearly, there's a lot of room for improvement—and that's great news, because it means that many of these ideas will be easy to implement in your own life. It's not about making sweeping changes across every room in your home, or getting your family to stop all their superconsumer habits and live like our pre-retail ancestors. Instead, as with all things (almost) zero waste, it's about making thoughtful decisions in your everyday life and planning carefully for bigger decisions in the future.

Your home should be the easiest place to start working toward an (almost) zero-waste lifestyle. Here, you don't need a to-go cup with a straw, or fourteen shopping bags to carry groceries, or sample-size shampoos to wash your hair. Unlike when you're at work, at school, at a restaurant, or out and about, you're not at the mercy of anyone else's decisions—you can choose recycled paper goods, control the thermostat, and decide for yourself how to manage your home and the life you've built there so that your impact on the planet is as comfortably small as you'd like it to be.

MAKE YOUR OWN ALL-PURPOSE CLEANING SOLUTION.

Want to eliminate a shelf full of household cleaning products in numerous plastic bottles and jugs? Many professional house cleaners swear by a water-dampened cloth and some muscle—yes, even to clean grimy windows. But if you're the type who likes to spritz a solution on counters, porcelain, and other surfaces, repurpose an old spray bottle and fill it with one part water to one part white vinegar. You can use the mixture as is or create a custom blend with a few drops of lemon essential oil or your favorite natural scent. For tough surface stains—even on granite—a paste of baking soda and water is also highly effective.

USE COTTON CLOTHS INSTEAD OF PAPER TOWELS.

Many cloth rag materials have environmental knocks against them. Microfiber towels are excellent at grabbing and holding dust and dirt particles—but they can shed microplastic fibers when washed (which then end up in rivers, oceans, and other bodies of water—and potentially in the digestive systems of the seafood we eat), and are not universally recyclable. Even cotton, a natural fiber, has come under scrutiny for its heavy reliance on chemical pesticides, large amounts of water, and vast farmland.[2] But when you reuse cotton that you already have in your home—an old T-shirt, a cut-up bedsheet or bath towel—you're offsetting the environmental burden created when that item was made, and sparing rolls upon rolls of paper towels in the process.

Ten Household Areas You Can Clean Using Just a Damp Cloth

- Windows
- Mirrors
- Woodwork trim (baseboards, windowsills, wainscoting)
- Blinds and shutters (wood and wood-look)
- Picture frames and glass
- Kitchen cabinets
- Countertops
- Porcelain sink
- Kitchen and bath tiles
- Stainless steel

USE 100 PERCENT CELLULOSE SPONGES.

Typical synthetic sponges are plastic-based, meaning they come with all the microplastic-shedding and live-forever baggage other plastics are known for. Considering that most experts recommend replacing your bacteria-laden kitchen sponge every two weeks to a month, that's a lot of waste going straight to the landfill just so you can clean your chef's knife. Instead, buy plant-based cellulose sponges. Made from wood pulp, these sponges are biodegradable and even compostable. To further reduce waste, look for cellulose sponges that are packaged minimally in a small paper or cardboard sleeve, rather than sealed in plastic film.

KILL WEEDS WITH BOILING COOKING WATER.

Why use water once when you can use it twice? Not only can cooking water be repurposed in other recipes (see "Eat and Cook (Almost) Zero-Waste" for ideas), you can also use it to kill weeds in sidewalks, driveways, and other places you don't want them to grow. Once you've removed your pasta or vegetables from the water, make sure it's still boiling before carefully taking it off the stove. Head outdoors and, taking care not to splash your feet or legs, pour the boiling water over the weeds. This method works best for standalone weeds growing in cracks in cement or asphalt; if you pour boiling water on weeds that are growing in the middle of your garden or grassy lawn, you'll kill both the unwanted plants and the good ones.

GET A RAIN CATCHER.

Indoor and outdoor plants can thrive on collected rain-water, even more so than tap water. Unlike the tap water in many areas, rainwater doesn't contain fluoride, chlorine, or other chemicals and minerals that can inhibit plant growth. Rain barrels can vary in size from thirty to one hundred gallons and are used to collect rainwater from gutter downspouts so you can use it to water plants and even to wash your car. Aside from providing a natural, untreated drink for your plants, collecting rainwater also helps conserve tap water, save money on your water bill, and reduce potential flooding of your property. You can find barrels made of upcycled plastic, stainless steel, ceramic, or wood; just be sure to check your state laws regarding rainwater collection, as some states have limits on residential water collection. For example, Colorado allows homeowners to use no more than two rain barrels, with a combined capacity of 110 gallons, to capture rainwater from their rooftops.[3]

Using Rainwater on Herb, Fruit, and Vegetable Gardens

There is no definitive, unanimous verdict on the safety of using collected rainwater on plants you plan to eat. Though some experts and home rainwater collectors worry that contaminants like lead, zinc, total coliform bacteria, polycyclic aromatic hydrocarbons, and even *E. coli* (from animal excrement) can accumulate in roof runoff and end up in rainwater barrels, a study conducted at Rutgers University[4] found that the rainwater collected from asphalt-shingle roofs contained low or no levels of all of the above contaminants (except *E. coli*). The recommendation, however, was that with the following proper care and water treatment, rainwater could be safely used on gardens harvested for food.

Here's what they suggest:

TREAT YOUR RAINWATER BARREL WITH BLEACH. Before you start collecting water, the research team advises cleaning the barrel with a 3 percent bleach solution. The formula they recommend is to add ⅛ teaspoon of unscented household bleach with a 5 to 6 percent chlorine solution per gallon of water. Once your barrel is clean, you also need to treat the water you collect with bleach; the study suggests that water in a typical fifty-five-gallon rain barrel should be treated with approximately one ounce of bleach, and that you should wait about twenty-four hours before using the water in your garden in order to allow the chlorine to dissipate.

KEEP COLLECTED RAINWATER OFF THE LEAVES AND FRUIT OF THE PLANT. The study's authors suggest using drip irrigation, which delivers the water directly to the soil.

WATER YOUR GARDEN IN THE MORNING, AND HARVEST LATER IN THE DAY. This will allow the leaves to dry and ultraviolet light to disinfect the plants.

MAKE THE SWITCH FROM DISPOSABLE PLASTIC ZIP-TOP BAGGIES.

It's hard. They're so convenient, and for many of us, they've been a part of our lives for so long. But in the ranks of single-use plastics, disposable zip-top bags (snack size, sandwich size, quart, gallon . . .) are right up there with straws. Luckily, there are other great options for when you need to stash snacks, meals, toiletries, or even phone chargers. Metal tins, Mason or other glass jars, and bamboo containers are all useful. But when you truly want a zip-top bag for your lunch, leftovers, or small household items, a reusable silicone bag is a good, eco-friendlier option. While silicone isn't biodegradable, it *is* nontoxic, it doesn't break down in extreme temperatures, and it's extremely durable. So if you need to decide between going through a box of forty-five plastic bags a week or buying one silicone bag and keeping it for decades, know that getting the silicone is better and less wasteful. You can find leak-proof and washable zip-top silicone baggies in different sizes to fit all your needs.

USE RECYCLED, COMPOSTABLE PAPER NAPKINS.

How many napkins do you use during a meal? Even if you limit yourself to just one, over the course of a year you would use 1,095 napkins. In ten years, that's 10,950 napkins. In a seventy-five-year lifetime, that's 82,125 napkins. (You know napkins come from trees, right?) If you're not already using paper napkins made from recycled paper (ideally, 100 percent recycled paper) and not whitened with chlorine bleach, it's a good idea to start doing so now. While paper napkins—like tissues and paper towels—aren't recyclable, they *are* compostable, as long as they aren't greasy or contaminated with chemicals from cleaning products. (One more reason to make your own all-natural cleaning spray—and use washable cloths for cleaning.)

BETTER YET, SWITCH TO (UPCYCLED) CLOTH NAPKINS.

By making napkins from scraps of cloth you already have—bed linens, denim, terry cloth, or frayed or stained cotton dish towels—you're not only cutting your reliance on paper napkins but also giving fabric a second life, thus reducing its environmental footprint. (Cotton, for example, is an incredibly resource-intensive fiber to grow and produce, zapping water and land and relying heavily on pesticides.) If you can sew a simple hem, by hand or by machine, you can make cloth napkins that you can use again and again—and even take with you to restaurants or when you eat your weekday desk lunch.

REPAIR, DON'T REPLACE.

If you want to go (almost) zero waste, try channeling your inner handyman whenever something breaks. The towel bar fell off the wall? You don't have to get a new one; learn how to repair it (you might want to use a wall anchor this time around, for example). Your coffee table is a little wobbly? Don't start shopping for a new one; grab a screwdriver, turn it over, and tighten the legs. Tired of staring at your dated, hand-me-down bedroom set? Some nontoxic paint stripper (or even just plenty of sandpaper) is all you need to prep the wood and get it ready for a new, modern (nontoxic) finish. Before you decide to replace any household item, do a little research to see if you can fix it or refurbish it first. Search for how-to videos on everything from using a drill to stopping a toilet from running (without buying a new part).

REPURPOSE EVERYTHING.

Get in the habit of looking at an unwanted item in your home and asking yourself *What else could I do with this?* Remove the top from a baby's changing table to create linen storage in a hallway. Repurpose an old side table as a useful nightstand. A chipped cereal bowl can make a pretty planter for succulents or a catchall for bangle bracelets. Cardboard gift and jewelry boxes make excellent junk-drawer organizers. Roomy, attractive out-of-season beach bags can hold spare bath towels in a guest bathroom. Scraps of fabric, wrapping paper, or wallpaper can be framed and hung on walls as art. Line an empty picture frame with sheet cork for a stylish home office corkboard. Once you start looking at objects with a fresh eye, their possibilities become endless.

GET CRAFTY WITH FOOD PEELS.

Dye fabrics (and Easter eggs) naturally with food scraps from beets (for shades of red and purple), avocado pits (pale pink), red cabbage (blue), onion skins (orange), and spinach (green). In some cases you can use a juicer to extract the colorful liquids, or simmer the scraps in water to release their color and then strain and reduce to concentrate the hue. (Compost any food solids that get strained out.)

BUY A HOUSE THAT'S BEEN LIVED IN BEFORE.

Tear-downs and new-construction homes are the opposite of zero waste. In just one year, 169.1 million tons of construction and demolition waste were generated, according to 2015 data from the EPA.[5] While cities and building manufacturers are implementing new procedures and policies to save more demolition materials for reuse and employ more environmentally friendly practices, the easiest zero-waste way to buy a home is to purchase one that's already been lived in by at least one owner. It's reuse on a large scale.

RENOVATE RESPONSIBLY.

Apply the "repair, don't replace" and "repurpose everything" filter to any home improvements you take on, large or small. Can you repaint the kitchen cabinets to suit your personal taste, rather than gutting the room and starting over? Can doorknobs be polished instead of changed? Would the chandelier that looks ostentatious in the dining room look fun and whimsical in a bedroom? Cast a creative eye on your surroundings and see how you can make use of existing materials to create a home that reflects your style.

When you can't renew items in your home, look for secondhand materials that might be perfect for your project. From bathtubs and sinks to flooring and cabinetry, there's an entire industry devoted to reselling pre-owned home supplies. There are companies that remove and resell entire kitchens—from the cabinets to the appliances—for less than retail, meaning you might score better-quality secondhand materials than you would have been able to afford otherwise. Not only do you get the benefit of a custom, new-to-you look but you've also saved these materials from the landfill.

Where to Source Secondhand Home Materials

- Garage sales
- Resale auction sites
- Live auctions
- Flea markets
- Online and live swap groups
- Habitat for Humanity's ReStore
- Junkyards and salvage stores
- PlanetReuse.com
- ReuseWood.org

CHOOSE LOW-IMPACT FLOORING.

Putting down new floors? Reclaimed hardwood makes for an eco-friendly and unique choice. Natural flooring like linoleum, wool or jute rugs, bamboo, and cork all make for more environmentally friendly choices as long as the adhesives, backing, and sealants used are low-VOC (volatile organic compounds). If you're going for newer materials like vinyl plank flooring or carpeting, shop for versions that have been made using recycled materials. Another option: instead of wall-to-wall carpeting, choose floating carpet tiles that connect to one another to create a unified look but that can easily be replaced one tile at a time in case of damage or staining.

MAKE WASTE SEPARATION EASY AND CONVENIENT.

Designate a centrally located spot for your paper, glass, metals, plastic film (like grocery bags, thin plastic packaging wrap, and dry cleaning bags), light bulbs, batteries, and any other materials that your community recycles. If you already own plastic containers, by all means keep using them. If you need to buy or obtain containers, look for ones made of 100 percent recycled plastic, or get creative with some of the ideas below. Whatever you choose, make sure your bins are large and easily accessible so that it becomes habit to place waste in the proper receptacle, rather than defaulting to throwing it into the trash bin.

Five Alternatives to Plastic Recycling Containers

- Wicker or woven grass baskets
- Galvanized metal buckets
- Laundry sacks
- Reusable shopping bags
  (the kind with flat bottoms)
- Wire rolling office carts

Buy recycled everything— starting with toilet paper.

Did you know that most commercial toilet paper is produced using old-growth trees from ancient forests? The NRDC launched a campaign urging Americans to "wipe right" and to sign a pledge to use sustainable and recycled toilet paper in order to preserve these and other forests used for TP.[6] According to the NRDC, if every American replaced just one roll of toilet paper made from virgin forest fiber with a 100 percent recycled-content TP roll, we'd save more than one million trees.

Check out this list of other popular household items that come in sustainable and/or recycled forms. (Here's hoping that by the time you read this, the list is even longer!)

- Toilet paper
- Paper towels
- Napkins
- Tissues
- Writing paper
- Wrapping paper
- Notebooks
- Pens
- Pencils
- Plastic trash bags
- Plastic bottles
- Aluminum cans
- Paper shopping bags
- Woven blankets
- Area rugs
- Doormats
- Carpeting
- Floor tiles
- Wallpaper
- Yoga mats

- Furniture
- Clothing
- Shoes
- Jewelry

Buy new things less often.

A zero-waste consumer mind-set might go something like this: *Do I need a new thing? Can I reuse or re-purpose something I already own? Could I obtain the thing secondhand? Could I borrow it from someone else (preferably someone local)?* The fewer new items you bring into your life, the less energy you'll need to spend figuring out how to dispose of them at the end of their life cycle.

Rethink your Internet shopping habit.

If you really need that item within the next twenty-four hours, is there any possibility you can walk or ride a bike to buy it locally rather than having it shipped? You'll be saving the fuel (and carbon emissions) required to fly or truck it from the warehouse to your doorstep, as well as the cardboard, plastic, and other packaging used to ship it. For those times when you do choose to shop online, here's how you can reduce waste:

- Choose the "pick up at local store" option. This is like the best of all worlds: you can browse via endless scroll from the comfort of your couch/bus ride home/

kitchen table, and then make a quick trip to pick up your purchase locally, thus saving shipping materials and the fuel it would have taken to deliver the item to your home.

- Don't accept the order in multiple shipments. Be sure to click (or unclick, depending on the situation) the box on the checkout page that says "This order may come in multiple shipments." Instead, opt to have everything packed and shipped at once. It may take slightly longer to get to you, but it will reduce the packaging and resources used to deliver it to you.

- Request "frustration-free" packaging. Amazon's Certified Frustration-Free Packaging program7 is available for many products on its site. When you choose this option, your package is shipped in easy-to-open recyclable materials, with minimal waste. (In other words, you won't get your palm-size item delivered in a boot-size box crammed with filler materials.) As this program becomes more popular with consumers, it's likely that other online retailers will follow suit.

REPLACE BURNED-OUT INCANDESCENT LIGHT BULBS WITH LED BULBS.

As the old-school light bulbs in your home die, replace them with energy-efficient LED bulbs. LEDs last longer, use less energy, and don't contain toxic mercury like CFLs (compact fluorescent light bulbs) do. According to the Department of Energy, Energy Star–rated LEDs use just 20 to 25 percent of the energy of traditional light bulbs, and last fifteen to twenty-five times longer.[8] That means less energy wasted, as well as fewer bulbs discarded over the course of a lifetime. LED light bulbs are available in a variety of colors and shades (both warm and cool), are often dimmable, and can be used indoors and outdoors. When your LED bulbs do eventually burn out, contact your local recycling center to dispose of them properly.

USE THE "OFF" SWITCH MORE OFTEN.

Turn off lights when you leave a room. Set your computer to sleep mode when you take a lunch break. Turn off the TV or radio when you leave the house. (Playing '90s alternative music isn't going to make your cat less lonely.[9]) The rules our parents enforced to save money on utility bills when we were kids still hold true—for your household budget and for the energy toll on our planet.

Open the shades.

Blackout shades are great for sleeping, but they're not helpful when you're putting on makeup in the morning. Heavy curtains may give a warm, cozy vibe to your living room, but they're terrible for reading on the couch. Lessen your reliance on artificial lighting by letting natural light illuminate your home. If you've got energy-efficient windows, there's no need to fear drafts, so open your shades, lift those blinds, pull back those curtains, and let the sun shine in.

Upgrade household appliances and other items efficiently.

Whenever you need to replace materials or appliances in your home—from old, drafty windows to the dishwasher—look for the least wasteful way to dispose of the unwanted materials, while also replacing them with the most sustainable and energy-efficient options. If you're working with a contractor on window replacement, for example, tell them you'd like them to dismantle the existing windows rather than demolishing them, so that the glass, wood, metal, or other materials might be recycled or reused. Then choose to install energy-efficient windows, which keep your house cooler in hot weather and warmer in cold weather, thus reducing the amount of electricity or gas needed to keep your home at a comfortable temperature. Likewise, appliances with an Energy Star rating use less energy than other (or older) models, lessening your personal energy consumption and lightening the strain on these resources in general.

WASH DISHES THE RIGHT WAY.

To clarify, here's the wrong way: letting the faucet blast hot water at full force while you individually wash each dish, pot, knife, and pan underneath the flow. You're literally pouring water—one of the planet's most precious natural resources—down the drain. Instead, fill the sink with warm, sudsy water, then turn off the faucet before washing a meal's worth of pots, pans, and utensils. If you have a double sink, fill the other side with clean, warm water for rinsing. (No double sink? A roomy, shallow bucket will also work.) If you'd rather use the dishwasher, make sure it's full before you run it; doing so makes the water used per item as minimal as possible. Energy-efficient dishwashers use about four gallons of water per load, and require a smaller amount of energy to heat the water and drive the water pump.

INVEST IN A PROGRAMMABLE THERMOSTAT.

Look, you're busy. Why put pressure on yourself to remember to raise your air-conditioner temperature from 78°F when you're home[10] to 85°F when you leave the house for the day? Wouldn't it be more convenient (and, let's be honest, more reliable) to let a programmable thermostat do the remembering for you, saving you time as well as energy? Come winter, you can program the thermostat to automatically drop from the recommended daytime heating temperature of 68°F down to an overnight level of 62 to 66°F, which is the suggested range for comfortable sleeping. Not only will you use fewer resources to heat and cool your home but you'll also save money—approximately $180 a year,[11] according to the EPA and Department of Energy's Energy Star guidelines.

PAINT A ROOM (OR ANYTHING) IN THE MOST SUSTAINABLE WAY POSSIBLE.

It's always worth searching your area to scout out recycled paint. It's also safe to mix different colors of latex paint together to create your own custom shade. If you're buying new paint, minimize the possibility of inhaling harmful, often hormone-disrupting chemicals or sending them down your drain and into the water supply during post-painting cleanup by looking for nontoxic, all-natural paint. Depending on your project, you might want to try eco-friendly, natural linseed oil paint. Since it can't be applied with a paint roller, you'll want to save it for smaller projects where you won't mind using a paintbrush. No- or low-VOC paint is another environmentally friendlier paint, though the solvents and additives used can still be harmful.

More Ways to Paint with Less Waste

CALCULATE YOUR PAINT NEEDS: Determine the square footage of the area you're painting, minus any doorways or windows, and then check the paint manufacturer's website (or ask where you buy your paint) to calculate how many gallons you'll need.

SKIP THE PLASTIC DROP CLOTH: Protect your floors, furniture, and anything else you want to remain splatter-free with an old sheet, newspapers, or slit-open paper grocery bags.

USE AN ECO-FRIENDLIER PAINT TRAY: Look for recycled-paper paint trays instead of the typical single-use plastic liners.

DISPOSE OF PAINT PROPERLY.

If you've ever used a can of latex or oil paint to paint your home, then there's probably a half-empty can still sitting somewhere in your home. Paint is notoriously hard to dispose of: you can't throw it away with non-recyclable trash, and you can't pour it down the drain. Oil paint is considered hazardous waste, and even though latex paint is not, there are still strict rules governing the disposal of unused and partially used cans. Happily, the paint industry, certain nonprofits, and local and state governments are working to improve your options for getting rid of paint you no longer need. PaintCare, a nonprofit organization created by the paint industry, runs paint collection sites in Oregon, California, Colorado, Minnesota, Connecticut, Rhode Island, Maine, Vermont, Washington, and the District of Columbia.[12] Habitat for Humanity ReStores will take latex paint in its original container, with its original label.[13] You can also go the FreeCycle.com route, offer paint to neighbors in a local social media group, or see if other organizations in your community could use it (like a school theater group, a community center, or a place of worship).

DON'T THROW OUT YOUR EXISTING PLASTICS.

Before you toss all the plastics in your home into the recycling bin in an effort to make a zero-waste clean sweep, consider whether it's better for the planet for you to keep using them, at least for a while longer. If that hard plastic flowerpot is uncracked and perfectly useful, there's no need to transfer your zinnia to a terra-cotta pot. Likewise, if the plastic bin storing your out-of-season clothing is still functional, you don't have to empty the contents now. Only 9 percent of all plastic ever produced has been recycled,[14] and we know that the plastic on the planet today will be with us for many generations to come (an estimated 450 to 1,000 years), so the least wasteful thing we can do at this point is put them to use as long as they're here.

GIVE UP CLAY KITTY LITTER.

Yes, it clumps neatly, making it easy to scoop. Yes, it masks the odor of pee and poop. But no, it's not biodegradable, so it will just sit in a landfill forever (alongside plastic water bottles and old lipstick tubes). Instead, try biodegradable litter made from recycled newspapers, corn, wheat, coconut, or wood. Many of these litters can be composted—though for non-food gardening only. Cat waste is considered toxic because it can contain parasites (which is one more reason to keep the neighbors' cats out of your vegetable garden). But if you have a separate compost heap for non-food fertilizing, it's possible to compost your kitty litter and waste. If not, simply dispose of it in a biodegradable trash bag and send it to the landfill, knowing you've at least minimized waste to the maximum of your ability.

CLEAN UP AFTER DOGS RESPONSIBLY.

There's an easy way to break your addiction to those little rolls of poop bags that conveniently snap onto your leash, ready anytime your dog pops a squat. Swap traditional plastic doggy bags for a compostable variety. Compostable bags will break down over months, if actually composted—but if you throw them in the trash, they'll sit in the landfill for years, anaerobically decomposing at a far slower rate. As with cat waste, you should use compost that contains dog waste only on non-food areas of your garden.[15] Another option? Pick up dog poop with newspaper, then drop it in the toilet and flush it once you're home.

GIVE UP GAS-POWERED LAWN EQUIPMENT.

An hour of gas-powered lawn mowing produces as much air pollution as a typical car driven for forty-five miles, according to the Minnesota Pollution Control Agency.[16] Swap out gas-guzzling leaf blowers and lawn mowers for electric types that use rechargeable battery packs—or, better yet, grab a rake or a push mower to burn only human energy.

PLANT SOMETHING OTHER THAN TURF GRASS.

Every year, the fifty million acres of turf grass lawns in the United States consume nearly three trillion gallons of water, two hundred million gallons of gas (for all that mowing), and seventy million pounds of pesticides, according to the NRDC.[17] But there are a number of less wasteful ways to cover your front or back lawn. Perhaps the lowest-maintenance option is to let your grass grow naturally—no regular mowing, no extra watering; just high, wild, free grass. But if you can't find the beauty in that look, or if your community has restrictions against it, there are other options:

- A wildflower lawn. Have you ever seen a gorgeous patch of wildflowers growing on the side of a highway and had the urge to go running through it? Now's your chance to grow one of your very own.
- A rock lawn. These super-low-maintenance lawns are especially popular in shore towns, where second-

homeowners aren't around often enough to care for green grass. A pebbly lawn can be accented with native plants that thrive in your local climate.

- A rain garden. This is especially useful if you live in an area prone to light flooding. A rain garden is a low-lying area of your yard filled with deep-rooted native grasses and perennials. When it rains, the water naturally collects in this garden, and the plants soak it up, keeping it from flooding your basement, walkway, or other areas.
- Groundcover plants. The magic is in their name: these plants quickly spread to cover as much ground as you're willing to give them. Depending on what part of the country you live in, you might choose Japanese sweet flag, Asian star jasmine, woodruff, lily of the valley, stonecrop succulents, or creeping herbs, such as thyme and oregano.18
- Ornamental grass. These grasses aren't meant to be mowed—they fluff up in beautiful tufts, sometimes creating the look of a uniform lawn.

SWAP LIQUID SOAPS FOR BARS AND POWDERS.

Bar soap isn't just for your bathroom. You can cut back on plastic by buying solid blocks of dishwashing soap, laundry detergent, and stain removers instead of their liquid counterparts. Taken individually, laundry and dishwasher pods are zero waste—they fully dissolve with use—but the cardboard or plastic packaging they typically come in is not.

STOP AUTOMATICALLY UPGRADING YOUR MOBILE DEVICES.

Yes, shiny new things are irresistible—until you need to figure out what to do with the old ones. Americans get rid of millions of cell phones every year, according to the EPA,[19] and a Gallup poll found that 44 percent of people upgrade their phones as often as their service providers allow, which is generally every two years.[20] When you do get rid of your phone or tablet, don't throw it out. Instead, consider giving it to someone else or donating it to charity (if it still works), sell it or trade it in for a new one, or recycle it at your local electronics recycling location (check with your town or city government to find out where it is).

GET CRAFTY WITH SCRAPS.

Whether you keep these scraps for your own creative pursuits or donate them to local schools to use in art class, save them from the trash bin and repurpose them as things of beauty.

- Cardboard paper towel and toilet paper rolls
- Buttons
- Crayon nubs (melt them down together for reuse)
- Scraps of cloth
- Broken dishes or pottery (for mosaic projects)
- Bottle caps
- Toothpaste tube caps
- Felt marker caps
- Cardboard packaging inserts
- Egg cartons
- Gift wrap
- Magazines
- Maps
- Construction paper scraps
- Costume jewelry

LEARN WHERE TO RECYCLE ANYTHING.

Earth911.com offers a recycling search guide for more than 350 materials, from latex paint to cell phone accessories. Simply type in the item you'd like to recycle, enter your zip code, and you'll get a list of locations near you that will accept the item for recycling.

OFFER YOUR FURNITURE TO OTHERS.

A whopping 9.69 million tons of furniture and furnishings went into landfills in 2015, according to the EPA.[21] That's a lot of outdated bar stools and dressers. But just because you're tired of that bleached-oak armchair or don't have the energy to reupholster your grandmother's couch doesn't mean someone else wouldn't be interested. Next time you've got a piece to unload, try these options before sending it to the dump.

- Ask everyone in your family. It's entirely possible that rather than see grandma's couch leave the family, your cousin will take it off your hands.
- Offer it to college kids. When you're furnishing your first off-campus apartment, you're usually not that picky.
- Ask teachers. Every so often, some lucky teacher gets a classroom big enough for

a love seat or other piece of furniture—maybe yours.

- Post it on a local resale site. Make a few bucks or give it away; either way, you win by sending it to a better place.

- Give it away on social media. Offering the furniture to your neighborhood group has extra benefits: you enjoy the goodwill of giving someone a piece they can use, and they don't have to travel far to pick it up.

- Donate it to a community center. It's always worth asking if your local community center or senior center needs a table/chair/couch.

- Put it at the curb a few days before bulk pickup. To be crystal clear, put a sign on it that says "Free." Some lucky passerby might decide it's just the thing for their home and take it off your hands.

THREE

Maintain (Almost) Zero-Waste Personal Care

Take a peek in your shower or bath—what do you see? If you're like most people, you'll find yourself staring at plastic bottles and tubes of body wash, conditioners, shampoos, and other personal-care items, plus maybe a plastic-handled razor or two, a plastic mesh shower puff, and plastic bath toys if you've got kids. Oh, and what about your shower curtain liner? Unless you specifically sought out a non-PVC type, it's likely made of vinyl.

It might feel as though your health, beauty, and

grooming routines only work because of the convenience of plastic and the flexibility of disposable items. When that shower puff gets mildewy or starts to smell, you can toss it and buy another. When your giant bottle of body wash runs out, you can recycle it and buy another. But given that beauty and personal care is an $89.5 billion industry (according to 2018 figures)[1], you can imagine how much waste we're collectively generating every time we run out of our favorite soaps, creams, lotions, and makeup.

There are ways to manage your personal care and reduce the amount of packaging—plastic or otherwise—used. An increasing number of manufacturers both large and small are experimenting with different packaging options, from using recycled materials to streamlining refill containers. And the beauty and personal-care industry isn't the only one floating new, more environmentally friendly approaches. The health and fitness world is paying as much attention to our planet's wellness as it is to ours. Here are different ways you can reduce waste in your personal-care and wellness habits.

GET A NEW (NON-DISPOSABLE) RAZOR.

One frequently cited statistic that dates back to 1990 is the EPA estimate that two billion disposable razors and blades are produced each year[2]—and likely end up in the landfill. That figure doesn't seem to have been updated in thirty years (over which time it's surely grown), but it's scary enough as it is. Because razor blades are sharp, and both the razors themselves and disposable blade cartridges are often made of metal and plastic, they aren't accepted for recycling. If you've been using disposable razors, it's time to invest in a less wasteful option. Try a safety razor made of metal, bamboo, or any number of sustainable materials. The stainless steel blades don't come encased in plastic, and many people swear by how easy these razors are to use, even on sensitive skin, and what a close shave they can give.

LET YOUR GRAYS GROW IN.

If you're looking for a zero-waste approach to hair color, embracing your natural shade is the most eco-friendly option out there. No more car trips to the salon for chemical hair dye applied with a plastic brush, out of a plastic mixing tray, from a formula that was shipped to the salon in a plastic squeeze bottle packed in a cardboard box; instead, let your original hair color grow in. (Truly, there is usually no more flattering hair color for your skin than the hue you already have.) Need inspiration? The Instagram account @grombre is dedicated to the growing-in process and features empowering and confidence-building stories of hair-color evolution.

. . . Or DIY your color with greener formulas. Not convinced that your natural shade is your best look? You still have options. For starters, look for hair-coloring products with naturally derived ingredients (Aveda's hair-color line, for example, is 95 percent naturally derived[3]) and no ammonia (which is corrosive and toxic at high levels) or p-phenylenediamine (which is derived from petroleum). If you're looking to dye your hair a shade in the red, brown, or black family, henna is a natural option. You can find powdered henna in bulk at some bulk-goods stores, and it also comes in bars, too. (Lush sells henna bars—in minimal packaging—in various shades.[4])

BUY BARS, NOT BOTTLES.

A big squirt of bath gel is nice, but bar soap can be just as luxurious. Shampoo in a tube is convenient, but a bar of shampoo is even more so—it will never spill in your overnight bag! In addition to solid body and face washes, you can find solid shampoo, conditioner, shaving soap, lotions, and deodorant, all in minimal packaging like reusable tins or recycled cardboard. It all comes down to water: you can buy your personal-care products in liquid form and packaged in plastic containers, or you can buy them in dry form and just add water yourself as needed.

READ SCRUB LABELS CAREFULLY.

A few years ago there was a lot of news about microbeads, which are tiny plastic-based beads used in face and body scrubs, cleansers, and bath products. These microbeads get swept down the drain, eventually released into our waterways, and mistaken for food by marine animals, who eat them. Bad news all around. But when microbeads left the headlines, it was easy to assume that personal-care manufacturers stopped using them. Unfortunately, that's not the case at all. Check the labels on your favorite products for ingredients that indicate microbeads are in the mix, like polyethylene (PE), polypropylene (PP), polymethyl methacrylate (PMMA), nylon (PA), polyurethane, and acrylates copolymer.[5]

REPLACE YOUR PLASTIC TOOTHBRUSH HABIT.

When it comes to the typical worn-out plastic toothbrush, there's really no good news at all, from a zero-waste perspective. For starters, it's probably not recyclable: it's too small for the recycling machinery and is likely made of composite materials that are difficult to separate.[6] Given that dentists advise changing toothbrushes every three months, an estimated one billion toothbrushes are disposed of each year in the United States. (And that's not counting the electric toothbrushes that go to the landfill, potentially leaking chemicals from their electronic insides.) However, bamboo toothbrushes are a better option—the sustainable material used for the handles is sometimes even compostable, though the nylon bristles used in most bamboo toothbrushes are not, so you'd have to rip them out before composting the handle. You can also find recycled-plastic toothbrushes, recycled-aluminum toothbrushes with replaceable heads from the Goodwell Company, or even wooden toothbrushes with pig-hair bristles that can be burned in a firepit or fireplace after they wear out.

USE TOOTHPASTE WITH MINIMAL PACKAGING.

Chances are, your curbside recycling pickup doesn't include toothpaste tubes. Even if your community recycles toothpaste tubes through a program run by Colgate and TerraCycle, you'd still need to rinse and dry the tube inside and out before putting it in your recycling bin. It's a worthy effort—but something requiring less effort and perhaps providing more positive impact would be to find alternate toothpaste solutions. Try some of these other options: chewable toothpaste tablets and tooth powder in recyclable packets or glass bottles, toothpaste in glass jars, or natural toothpaste in recyclable metal tubes.

RETHINK YOUR FLOSSING ROUTINE.

It's creepy how disposable plastic dental floss picks turn up in the weirdest places: retail parking lots, city streets, parks, beaches. Your first thought might be, *Who's flossing their teeth here?* But as you think about it some more, you might realize how easily those tiny, lightweight plastics can fall out of trash bags or recycling bins—and, of course, end up on our shores like so many other plastics we discard every year. Little plastic boxes of floss are less ubiquitous in public places but just as tricky to dispose of, as they often have a metal part that makes them nearly impossible to recycle. One closer-to-zero-waste option: Dental Lace refillable dental floss, which is made of silk, not plastic or plastic-coated thread, and comes in a refillable glass container with a stainless steel top. Other reduced-waste brands come in compostable cardboard containers instead of plastic ones. Another option is to use a water pick—aka an oral pulsating irrigator—which is a handheld electronic device that shoots a thin and powerful stream of water along the gum line and between teeth. There is, however, no research so far to determine whether a water pick is as effective at removing plaque from between teeth as floss is,[7] and you also have to consider how to dispose of your water pick when it eventually stops working or you grow tired of it.

GIVE UP BABY WIPES— FOR EVERYONE IN THE HOUSEHOLD.

Over the years, baby wipes have left the nursery, as people of all ages have embraced the extra-clean feeling that comes from using "flushable" wipes. But neither the packaged wet wipes meant for diapering babies nor the personal-care wipes meant for backsides of all ages are environmentally friendly. Researchers at Ryerson University in Ontario, Canada, tested 101 single-use wipes—23 of which were promoted as "flushable"[8]—and found that none of them was able to fall apart or disperse safely through the sewer system. And if these wipes—many of which contain plastic fibers—aren't degrading in water, there's no reason to expect them to degrade in any reasonably speedy way in a landfill. For babies, try keeping a stack of soft organic cotton or bamboo cloths or washcloths (or even repurposed bed-sheets or old cotton T-shirts) on hand that you can wet or dampen to use, and then machine wash in the same load with the cloth diapers. You could also do the same for the adults in the house, keeping a small lidded trash can in the bathroom for used cloths.

CHOOSE OTC PILLS IN BOTTLES, NOT BLISTER PACKS.

While it's always most important to choose the medication that's most effective for you and whatever condition you're trying to treat, your second consideration should be the packaging it comes in. There's generally little or no choice when it comes to prescriptions, which by law must be packaged and labeled according to accepted federal standards.[9] But there are ways to reduce your prescription packaging waste. When filling a prescription, it's always worth asking your pharmacy to skip the bag and just hand you the bottle and the informational printout, if necessary. And when it comes to over-the-counter drugs, a glass or plastic bottle of tablets is easier to reuse or recycle when empty than a box filled with individually foil-packed pills.

SOAP UP WITH A WASHCLOTH.

Nylon mesh loofahs may give good suds, but they trap bacteria and mildew, prompting experts to recommend they be replaced every few months . . . which means if you use them properly, you're sending four or more straight to the landfill every year, where they'll live forever. A better option? Washcloths in the sustainable, low-impact fabric of your choice (organic cotton, bamboo, and lyocell are all good options). Cloths should be changed a few times a week (and your bath towel once a week),[10] so be sure to stock up so that you can wash a full load of cloths and towels come the weekend.

MAKE YOUR OWN SHEET MASKS.

Who says (almost) zero-wasters can't embrace trends? Instead of buying single-use sheet masks for your face, try creating your own custom sheet mask out of an old pillowcase, T-shirt, or handkerchief. Cut a square of cloth slightly larger than your face, then drape it over your face and, with a non-waterproof makeup pencil, trace around your face, just inside your hairline. Then trace around your mouth and eyes and mark where your nostrils are. Remove the cloth, cut out holes where marked, and place the mask back over your face and adjust as needed to get the right fit. Now that you have a template, you can make a few masks to keep on hand. When you're ready for a mask, simply saturate it with the treatment of your choice, whether store-bought or DIY.

DIY Sheet Mask Treatments

For each formula, use roughly equal amounts of each ingredient—just enough to create a mixture that will saturate your mask.

MOISTURE MASK: oat milk

EXFOLIATING MASK: pineapple juice, lemon juice, and white grape juice

SOOTHING MASK: strong chamomile tea

ANTIOXIDANT MASK: honey, yogurt, and turmeric powder

GLOW MASK: honey and orange juice

POST-SUN MASK: natural aloe

CHOOSE BEAUTY BRANDS THAT MAKE AN EFFORT.

Traditional plastic compacts and lipstick tubes often have metal components, making them ineligible for most recycling programs, but there are more efficient ways to strive toward zero waste when it comes to your makeup and skin-care routine. Many beauty brands are using recyclable and compostable packaging; experimenting with recycled materials, including plastics, cardboard, and aluminum, as well as sustainable bamboo, glass, and plastic resin derived from corn;[11] and offering re-usable containers and refills for their products. Just a few of the brands making strides in this area are Aether Beauty, Antonym Cosmetics, Au Naturale Cosmetics,

Axiology, Bésame Cosmetics, Elate Cosmetics, Faraday Face, Ilia Beauty, Kjaer Weis, Lush, RMS Beauty, Sappho New Paradigm, Tata Harper, and Vapour Beauty.

USE SCENTS THAT MAKE SENSE.

It's estimated that perfumes, body sprays, and other personal scents typically contain a dozen or more potentially hazardous synthetic chemicals, including petrochemicals, which are derived from petroleum and create greenhouse gases.[12] It's hard to do the research on your favorite scent, though, because fragrance companies aren't legally required to disclose the ingredients in their products. The good news is that there are an increasing number of companies devoted to creating natural scents from sustainable ingredients, in recyclable and refillable packaging, with fully transparent ingredient lists. Whether you choose fragrances made from essential oils or ones that come in solid form in recyclable tins, your signature scent should make you feel as great as you smell.

REDUCE PERIOD-RELATED WASTE.

If you're currently using traditional menstrual pads and tampons, you may be interested to know that there are actually many ways you can work toward having a zero-waste period. From an eco-friendly perspective, conventional tampons aren't great. They're made with bleached, non-organic cotton (a material that requires a huge amount of natural resources and pesticides to produce), and some contain dyes as well.[13] And if your usual brand is packaged in plastic applicators wrapped in plastic wrappers and tucked inside a cardboard box . . . you can see how the waste adds up. For a baby step, try transitioning to a cardboard applicator—or, better yet, a brand with no applicator. Take it a step further by switching to an organic brand, like o.b. organic, LOLA, Rael, or Veeda (to name just a few). Many of these offer mail-order subscriptions, while others can be purchased at your local drugstore. Most offer pads, too. If you *really* want to step away from disposable period products, though, period panties and reusable cotton pads are two other ways to go. The idea is the same: the fabric absorbs the blood while you're wearing it, and then you remove, rinse, wash, and wear again. Fans of period panties swear they don't encounter leaks or icky feelings, but if you're skeptical, you can always try a more time-trusted method: the menstrual cup. You insert this flexible silicone or latex rubber cup much like a tampon, and it suctions to the vaginal walls, collecting blood before it leaves your body. You can leave it in for up to twelve hours, and then remove, empty, wash with soap and water, and reinsert.

SEEK OUT SUSTAINABLE WORKOUT CLOTHES.

More and more athletic-apparel brands are using post-consumer recycled materials, organic cotton, low-impact dyes, and eco-friendly packaging, making it less wasteful to replace your favorite running tights or bike shorts when they finally fall apart. Patagonia, Satva, Alternative Apparel, and Boody are just some of the brands manufacturing workout and athleisure clothing with an eye toward impact. Other companies are rolling out pieces within their existing lines using sustainable practices. Athleta's SuperSonic tights, for example, are made of recycled nylon and spandex. Check the labels before you buy, and if your favorite brand hasn't implemented any sustainable or lower-waste measures, let them know that it matters to you.

CREATE A HOME GYM WITH HOUSEHOLD ITEMS.

A good sweat shouldn't have to cost money or involve special equipment. While one could argue that joining a fitness club is zero-waste because you're buying a service, not a product, the fact is that club needs to fuel its heat, AC, and electricity; wash used towels; and frequently replace worn or outdated equipment (or run the risk of losing members, which would make all other operational efforts even more wasteful on a resources-per-person basis). Instead, utilize objects in your home environment to get a challenging workout. The following are just a few ideas; take a good look around your own home to come up with even more smart multitasking moves.

- Become a stair master. Lace up those running shoes and take the stairs—up and down—until you feel the burn. Need a bigger challenge? Try taking them two at a time, at the same speed.
- Use a kitchen chair as leverage. Tricep dips, lunges, planks—these muscle toners and more can all be done using a hard (not upholstered) chair or bench.
- Slide on towels. Sliders can maximize the intensity of core moves like mountain climbers and plank jacks—and on a smooth, solid surface, towels work just as well as purpose-built equipment.
- Use full beverage holders as weights. Fill two equally sized, clean, and dry beverage containers with dried beans or rice, screw the lids on tight, and then lift. (Too heavy? Remove some beans, then work up to a full bottle in each hand.)

REPURPOSE AN OLD YOGA MAT.

Many yoga mats are made from petroleum-based PVC (polyvinyl chloride) and rendered flexible with phthalates, which are known hormone disruptors. PVC isn't easily recyclable—you can't toss it into your plastics bin and leave it at the curb—and what's worse, once PVC hits the landfill, it can leak chlorine, carcinogens, and other toxic chemicals into the soil and air.[14] So if you have an old PVC yoga mat, do all you can to extend its life and keep it from doing harm to the environment. Here are a few ideas:

- Donate it to charity. If your mat is in good condition, either donate it to a local charity or see if the neighborhood community center or senior center can use it.
- Give it to an animal shelter. Check with area shelters to see if they accept yoga mats for bedding or to line crates.
- Use it in the garden. A yoga mat makes a generous, foldable knee pad that you can easily hose down.
- Bring it to the beach. Throw it down in the sand to lie on, and save your towel for drying off.

- Take it on a picnic. A yoga mat provides a more stable surface over grass than a sheet or a blanket.
- Use it for sleepovers and camping. It offers a little extra padding between the ground and your sleeping bag.
- Turn it into a car liner. For transporting potted plants, pets, muddy boots, wet surfing gear . . .
- Use under pet food and water bowls. Cut it to fit so spills are contained.

BUY A NEW, SUSTAINABLE YOGA MAT.

If your current mat is good for your practice, stick with it. But when you need a new one, look for a mat made of natural rubber or jute, which are biodegradable materials that don't off-gas volatile compounds.

FOUR

Travel Near and Far with (Almost) Zero Waste

Travel has a huge impact on the planet. In 2017, the EPA reported that transportation accounted for 29 percent of total greenhouse-gas emissions in the United States,[1] beating out electricity by one percentage point as the largest share of the problem. A typical passenger car emits about 4.6 metric tons of carbon dioxide per year, says the agency. A nonstop, round-trip flight in coach from Newark Airport to Los Angeles emits about 1.3 metric tons, according to MyClimate.org's CO_2 calculator. (That calculation goes up if you fly business or first class, and also if you have a connecting flight.)

It's enough to make you want to walk everywhere. Of course, then you'd wear out your shoes that much faster, requiring you to dispose of and then replace them. Likewise, biking, skateboarding, rollerskating—any mode of transportation you can think of—would eventually require you to get at least one part replaced.

So strive for (almost) zero waste. If you can walk or ride a bike literally everywhere, then do it more often. But if you can't, use common sense. Take public transportation whenever possible, and save on fuel in other ways where you can. Be efficient when it comes to travel gear and travel plans. Utilize whatever tips and strategies fit with your lifestyle during your trips to work, to visit family and friends, and to explore the world.

WEAR COMFORTABLE SHOES WHEN WALKING.

Real talk: if you can't walk a block in those shoes, you know you're going to end up driving (or asking someone else for a lift). So save yourself the CO_2 expenditure and make sure all the shoes you own are comfortable enough to walk in. Can't let go of your less practical favorites? Stash a pair of sneakers in your tote so you can slip them on and then skip the bus, subway, or hired ride.

USE MORE PUBLIC TRANSPORTATION.

The math just makes sense: subways and heavy rail trains produce on average 76 percent fewer greenhouse-gas emissions per passenger mile than an average single-occupancy vehicle (aka your car); light rail systems produce 62 percent fewer greenhouse gases, and bus transit produces 33 percent fewer, according to a report from the Federal Transit Administration.[2] Spare the planet the greenhouse gases and air pollution—and save yourself the stress of driving—and take public transportation whenever you can. That means when getting around your town or commuting to work, and also when traveling out of town. There's no better way to experience another city like a local than by taking their metros, trains, and buses.

OR CARPOOL.

Which sounds like more fun: Monday morning commute, or Monday morning mini road trip? If you're all going to the same place—the office, Back-to-School Night, the climate change rally—why not go together and reduce your overall carbon footprint? Census data from 2017 shows an uptick in carpooling among the top eleven US metropolitan areas.[3] Even nondrivers can get in on this pollution-reducing strategy by choosing the ride-share option in their favorite car-for-hire app. For every extra person in that car, you've just kept one more vehicle off the road.

Ride your bike.

A distance that might seem insurmountable on foot can seem incredibly doable on two wheels. A sixteen-mile round-trip journey to buy your favorite local honey? No big deal. Just strap on a helmet (and a backpack, for carrying purchases) and hit the road. The only energy used in biking is your own, which means you've just gotten a nearly-zero-waste workout, too. A double win for you and the planet.

Get an electric or hybrid car.

According to the US Department of Energy, transportation accounts for nearly three-fourths of all American petroleum consumption.[4] Switching to a hybrid or electric vehicle will help bring that number down, lowering the United States's reliance on petroleum, releasing less CO_2 into the atmosphere, and reducing our collective current rate of greenhouse-gas production. The money you'll save on gas? Consider it a bonus. If you're buying a new fully electric car, the savings don't end there. The federal government offers tax credits ranging from $2,500 to $7,500 on new electric car purchases (the rate varies depending on vehicle size and battery capacity).[5] Many states offer incentives, too—including cash rebates, additional tax credits, access to HOV lanes, and reduced toll fees.[6]

MAXIMIZE YOUR FUEL EFFICIENCY.

If you do drive a vehicle that relies entirely or partially on gas to run, make sure you're burning as little fuel as possible. This one's super easy—basically, just drive like a grown-up. Don't brake hard, accelerate hard, or speed wildly, and maintain a steady rate whenever possible. Also, keep the trunk empty when you can: the more weight in your car, the more fuel it requires to move. So while it might seem like a good idea to consistently keep your trunk full of beach gear (or fishing gear, tailgating gear, or hiking gear) for spontaneous day trips, it's actually not the most eco-friendly move.

TURN OFF YOUR ENGINE.

Many states have laws prohibiting keeping your motor running while parked, with heavy fines (into the thousands) if you get caught doing it. It's for good reason: according to the US Department of Energy,[7] personal vehicles generate around thirty million tons of CO_2 every year just by idling. By some estimates, if we all stopped idling, it would be equivalent to taking five million vehicles off the road.[8]

CHECK YOUR TIRE PRESSURE.

Whether you're driving a two- or four-wheeled vehicle, maintaining proper tire pressure not only makes driving safer but also extends the life of your tires and can increase fuel efficiency (less fuel = less pollution and greenhouse-gas emissions). According to the US Department of Energy,[9] you can improve your gas mileage by up to 3 percent by keeping your tires inflated to the proper PSI (pounds per square inch). Check the inside of the driver's door or the owner's manual for your car's recommended PSI.

BOOK DIRECT FLIGHTS.

It's a catch-22: you want to experience different cultures, see different parts of the world, and immerse yourself in humanity in all its variety—and yet to travel any great distance, you likely need to catch a plane, an act that helps pollute our planet, putting Earth and its every living inhabitant in peril. Of all the transportation-related greenhouse emissions in the United States, aircraft are responsible for 12 percent.[10] Instead of resigning yourself to streaming travel documentaries on your laptop from the comfort of your couch, fly smarter. Step one: book direct flights. The most jet fuel is wasted during takeoff and landing (taxiing is the biggest offender in the process[11]), so the more times you do that in one trip, the greater the environmental cost of your journey. Yes, it might be more expensive than taking a connecting flight, but consider it a small price to pay for extending the health of our planet and the people on it (including yourself).

Skip the upgrade.

It's simple math: You can fit more coach seats in an airplane than business or first-class seats, which means that the more passengers there are on the plane, the smaller each person's carbon footprint will be. Research from the World Bank[12] found that the footprint per mile for business and first classes is "substantially greater" than that of economy class, so if you fly coach, you'll not only save money but you'll also be a greenhouse-gas-emission-reducing hero. (And keep your heroism in mind the next time the passenger in front of you reclines their seat right into your lap. Think: *I'm saving the planet. I'm saving the planet. I'm saving the planet.*)

Buy carbon offsets.

In an effort to make your trip carbon-neutral, you can also turn to carbon offsets. The idea here is that you've reduced your environmental impact in all ways possible but still want to make up for the rest; so, basically, you spend money to fund a project that reduces greenhouse emissions—whether that's planting trees, landfill-gas capture, or wind power. Some airlines even have programs that help you calculate your CO_2 footprint per flight and then choose to support a project through the organizations they've partnered with—and if you're flying internationally, soon the burden won't be fully on you. A UN agree-

ment called CORSIA[13] has called for airlines themselves
to start offsetting their international flights by 2021.[14]

DON'T BUY TRAVEL-SIZE TOILETRIES.

When you travel, be sure to bring the same reduced-
plastics mentality that you apply to your daily grooming
routine. Rather than buy mini packaged versions of your
favorite soaps, shampoos, lotions, and other personal-
care items, portion some of your at-home favorites into
small metal reusable travel bottles and tins. Or, if you've
already got a shelf full of mini toiletries taking up space
in your cabinet, use them until they're empty—then refill them again and again, to keep them out of the not-
so-efficient plastic recycling stream or landfill.

PACK LIGHTLY.

There are many theories as to why airlines charge passengers for traveling with extra bags. When the fees were first
implemented, the price of jet fuel was to blame. Today,
some skeptics suggest that it's just a revenue stream airlines don't want to give up, especially since we've all gotten used to paying. Either way, the fees are here to stay.
But if that isn't enough to make you reconsider packing
that fifth pair of shoes, remember that the more luggage
you bring on the plane, the larger your individual carbon footprint. So, bring only what you'll need, make sure
shoes do double duty for different outfits and activities,

and call ahead to find out if there are hair dryers or beach towels available where you're staying. Not only will you be treading more lightly from an environmental-impact perspective but you'll also skip the extra baggage fees and lighten your load when zipping through airports or hauling your luggage up stairs or onto the hotel shuttle bus.

How to Streamline Your Packing List

CHECK THE WEATHER REPORT. Sorry to bring it up, but with climate change disrupting what we think of as "typical" weather in a given location at a certain time of year, it always makes sense to check the weather forecast for your destination ahead of time. This way you'll know whether to pack your raincoat, your bathing suit, or both.

PICK A COLOR THEME. Black, white, and red? Denim and neutrals? Shades of gray? Make sure every piece of clothing you pack can be worn with anything else in your suitcase so you'll have the maximum number of outfit combos for any occasion or weather.

BRING ONE LESS THAN YOU THINK YOU NEED. If you've set aside multiples of particular items of clothing or accessories, practice paring down. Nine pairs of underwear for a six-day trip? Take eight. Four pairs of jeans? Consider whether three might suffice. Two pairs of boots—one chunky, one stiletto? Just choose one. Unless you're already skilled at packing light, apply the "one less" rule to your entire suitcase.

STASH SOME LINGERIE WASH IN YOUR BAG. The "one less" rule will be easier to follow if you know you can hand-wash any item you want in the bathroom sink. On second thought, maybe *five* pairs of underwear are enough . . .

KEEP TRAVEL NECESSITIES ON HAND. Make room in your backpack or tote for these supplies to stay (almost) zero waste on the go:

- Refillable beverage container that can handle hot and cold drinks
- Reusable straw
- Reusable utensils

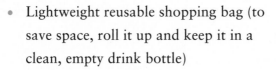

- Silicone zip-top bag (to hold clean or dirty straw/utensils, leftover snacks, etc.)
- Lightweight reusable shopping bag (to save space, roll it up and keep it in a clean, empty drink bottle)

OPT OUT OF RECEIPTS.

Get in the habit of declining paper receipts at the register, whether you're buying an apple at the train station or checking out of your hotel. Typical thermal-paper receipts are coated with BPA (Bisphenol A), an endocrine-disrupting chemical that, according to the National Institutes of Health,[15] plays a role in female and male infertility, early puberty, breast and prostate cancer, and metabolic disorders, including polycystic ovary syndrome (PCOS). One study found that BPA from receipts can be absorbed through your skin during typical handling.[16] Not only that, but if you recycle these receipts, it's possible that traces of BPA will be recycled along with them—possibly into items like napkins, toilet paper, or other materials that will once again come into contact with your skin. Luckily, skipping the receipt is becoming easier: many vendors—from pharmacies and department stores to restaurants and resorts—will ask if you'd like a receipt e-mailed or texted to you instead.

WORK FROM HOME.

If you have the option of working from home, try doing it more often. Think of all the resources you could conceivably save:[17]

- Water (skip the shower)
- Coffee to-go cup (no temptation to get a paper cup and plastic lid on the way to the office)
- Dry-cleaning solvent (no need to dry-clean your casual WFH clothes)
- Fuel for the commute
- Commute-related noise and air pollution
- Electricity to light the office (those office overheads are surely more energy-sucking than your home office LED bulb)
- Gas to heat the office (unlike most workplaces, you're in full control of the thermostat at home)
- Desk space
- Office supplies (no need to photocopy that report and walk it to your colleague's desk)

. . . and you could probably think of more resources unique to your work and living situation. The point is, businesses are catching on to the fact that telecommuting has many benefits—to the worker, to the company, and to the environment. There's less emphasis on the IRL, face-to-face experience when workers can be connected to their colleagues no matter where they're located. In fact, Darby Hoover of the NRDC says that for that organization, investing in a good video-conferencing system was a great way to connect staff who were already spread out across the country and around the world.

FIVE

Build an (Almost) Zero-Waste Wardrobe

As a culture, we're kind of clothes junkies. The newer, the fresher, the trendier, the better—and then once a piece is worn out, or just played out, we get rid of it. And while the EPA estimates that 14.2 percent of clothing and footwear was recycled in 2015 (the most recent year for which the agency has data), an estimated 10.5 million tons of textiles went into landfills that same year.[1] We have a long way to go to get to zero waste.

What's worse, garment-related waste starts even before you rip the tags off a new item. In her article "Waste Couture: Environmental Impact of the Clothing Industry,"[2] author Luz Claudio notes that the "demand for man-made fibers, especially polyester, has nearly doubled in the last fifteen years, according to figures from the Technical Textile Markets." The manufacturing of these synthetic fabrics, continues Claudio, requires

> large amounts of crude oil and releasing emissions including volatile organic compounds, particulate matter, and acid gases such as hydrogen chloride, all of which can cause or aggravate respiratory disease. Volatile monomers, solvents, and other by-products of polyester production are emitted in the wastewater from polyester manufacturing plants. The EPA, under the Resource Conservation and Recovery Act, considers many textile manufacturing facilities to be hazardous waste generators.

Synthetic fabrics are not the only materials with an unfriendly environmental profile. Cotton requires chemicals and vast amounts of water and other resources to produce; organic cotton might use fewer chemicals, but it still requires water, land, and other natural resources to grow. Bamboo is a sustainable resource, but turning it into the soft fabric we've come to know requires harmful chemical solvents like lye and carbon disulfide.[3] The takeaway? There is no one perfect fabric to choose when it comes to a zero-waste, environmentally friendly wardrobe. Not yet, anyway.

But building an (almost) zero-waste wardrobe is doable. As with any zero-waste efforts, it's a matter of gradually reducing your impact when it comes to clothing, accessories, and shoes, and exploring all available options to keep your discarded items out of the landfill. Of the many ideas here, you should find at least a few that fit your style.

CREATE A CAPSULE WARDROBE.

This tactic has a double benefit: fewer choices mean less decision fatigue—and more time in your day, since you won't find yourself standing blank-faced in front of an open closet, trying to figure out what to wear. A capsule wardrobe is one filled with just a few key pieces of good quality, in classic styling and neutral colors (or bold—just make sure they all coordinate). You should be able to combine these pieces in different configurations to create multiple looks across seasons and years. With a capsule wardrobe as your foundation, you can update your look from season to season with accessories (a vintage scarf, say) without completely discarding your clothing for newer, trendier pieces every few months. Capsule wardrobes are individual, depending on your preferences (skirts and dresses?), your lifestyle (traditional suits?), and where you live, but this list is a good starting point:

- Black pants
- Jeans
- Shorts
- Blazer
- White T-shirt
- Black T-shirt
- White button-down
- Trench coat
- Denim jacket
- Sweater
- Leggings
- Skirt
- Dress

Buy secondhand whenever you can.

From rummage sales to designer consignment sites, there are more opportunities than ever before to score pre-owned clothing, shoes, and accessories at every price point and style. Whether you're looking for one-of-a-kind vintage finds or high-end fashion pieces you might not otherwise be able to afford, extending the life of secondhand items not only keeps them out of the landfill but also reduces the overall demand for new items. And as more of us start turning away from the brand-new, cheaply made trendy items known as fast fashion, it will send a powerful message to the clothing and textile industry that consumers are hungry for more sustainable options.

Check the ingredients in your vegan leather.

Yes, some innovative new vegan leather is made from pineapple skins, cork, coated canvas, or even mushroom caps.[4] But the majority of vegan leather items are made from polyvinyl chloride (PVC) or polyurethane—in other words, plastic. (Years before it was called vegan leather, it was called "pleather": plastic leather.) If you're shopping for a leather-look jacket, shoes, or handbag, check the label to see exactly what it's made from. Even better, shop secondhand stores and websites for vegan leather, and give an older piece an extended life far away from the landfill.

DONATE ONLY WHAT'S STILL WEARABLE.

It's so tempting to take every last article of clothing you no longer want and send it off to your favorite charity. But some items shouldn't be donated at all. There's an easy way to decide whether that shirt or those shoes are worthy of the donation bin. Ask yourself, *Is it holey? Stained? Worn down? Irreparably smelly?* If you couldn't imagine someone else wearing the item in public with their head held high, find another way to dispose of it. Clothing and other donations should always be in good condition—too big or small for you, maybe, or no longer your style, but still wearable.

MAKE SURE YOUR CLOTHING GOES WHERE IT'S NEEDED.

At this point, there's a global surplus of donated secondhand clothing, partly because of the fast fashion trend, in which consumers cycle through wardrobes at a faster rate than ever before, discarding last season's items in favor of newer pieces. What's more, in the past few years, a number of East African countries have launched efforts to ban imported secondhand clothing and shoes.[5] In an effort to help boost their economies and create job opportunities, these countries want to develop their own clothing industries instead of living off other countries' discards.

With fewer communities of people truly in need of used clothing, the most responsible thing you can do is make sure you're donating items that will find a second life with someone else instead of ending up in storage and then being burned or dumped in a landfill. Contact your local churches or synagogues, community outreach centers, and homeless or women's shelters to see what their donation needs are, or donate to national organizations that either give items directly to those in need—like Dress for Success and Donate My Dress—or sell the items at secondhand stores and use the proceeds to assist others, like the Salvation Army, Goodwill, and Vietnam Veterans of America.

LEARN TO SEW—OR FIND A GOOD TAILOR.

Knowing how to hem a too-long dress or take in too-big pants is useful when you're shopping secondhand, and also when you want to keep wearing favorite clothes in your existing wardrobe. Sewing a button, darning a hole, taking in a waist, letting a hemline up or down . . . these are all simple sewing tasks that you can easily master by hand with just a needle and thread, or—even faster and easier—with a basic sewing machine. Of course, if you're not the DIY type, you can spend a little money for basic alterations at a reputable tailor and walk out with a custom-fitted wardrobe.

HOST A CLOTHING SWAP.

You've heard the rule, right—if you haven't used any item in the past three months, you probably don't need it in your life? Apply that basic principle to your wardrobe at the start of every season, but adapt it according to the time of year. Did you wear that sweater at all last winter? If not, you likely won't wear it this winter, either. Cull what no longer suits you, and then set a date and invite friends to a clothing-swap party. Everybody walks away with something new to them, along with the satisfaction of knowing they've saved clothes, shoes, and accessories from the landfill. Here's how to organize a clothing swap:

- Set guidelines. The idea is that the clothes, shoes, and accessories everyone brings should still be in good condition and stylish.
- Keep the guest list modest. Depending on

where you're hosting the gathering—a tiny studio apartment or a more spacious home—you want enough of a group that there will be variety, but not so many that you don't have room to display the items. Think seven to fifteen people.

- Designate stations. Clothes on one side of the room, shoes on the other, accessories in the hallway. Spread things out a bit so people have space to browse.
- Please everyone. Or at least try, by making sure there are at least two people of roughly the same clothing or shoe size at the gathering. (Otherwise, who will your six-foot friend swap with?)
- Create an exchange system. Make it easy: for every piece someone brings, they get to choose a piece to take home.
- Provide changing areas and lots of mirrors. A swap party works best when people are shopping and trying on and deciding simultaneously; things slow down if it's one at a time.
- Offer light snacks and drinks. It's a party, after all. Just keep things simple—and skip the red wine. It stains.
- Donate unwanted items to charity. At

the end of the party, offer to gather up whatever's left and donate it to a worthy cause.

Buy from sustainable brands.

When you do purchase new items, make sure your money is going where your heart is by shopping sustainable brands. These days, companies aren't shy about sharing their latest environmental and sustainability initiatives. If you're interested in a brand, check their website to see what they're doing to reduce their impact on the planet. Here are just a few examples of some of the good work being done by responsible brands:

- Reformation uses their "RefScale" to track the environmental footprint of each item they sell, calculating the pounds of carbon dioxide emitted, gallons of water used, and pounds of waste generated in making their clothing and shoes versus traditionally made garments.
- UK-based People Tree is Fair Trade Certified, meaning they not only make sure the workers involved in every step of their garment production are treated fairly but they also use organic cotton (thus reducing the amount of toxic pesticides in

the environment) and natural and low-impact dyes in their fabrics.

- Patagonia is Fair Trade Certified as well, and is committed to using sustainable materials whenever possible. Additionally, they encourage consumers to repair items rather than replace them, with the "Repair & Care" guides on their site—for everything from how to fix an unthreaded drawstring to how to repair a baffle on a down jacket.

- Allbirds crafts their shoes from a sustainably sourced combination of merino wool and eucalyptus tree fibers, uses recycled plastic bottles in their laces, and ships their products in 90 percent recycled cardboard packaging.

TAKE GOOD CARE OF YOUR SHOES.

The better you treat your footwear, the longer each pair of shoes will last, whether they're a cheap pair you bought on a whim or a pricey splurge you hope to be buried in.

- Conventional wisdom says that running shoes should be replaced every three hundred to five hundred miles, but caring for them properly will help put you closer to the five-hundred-mile mark. Hand-washing sneakers keeps the fabric clean and fresh and protects soles from the battering they'd get even on the gentle cycle in the washing machine. And, yes, let them air-dry.

- Store all shoes in a cubby, box, or shoe bag to keep them from getting dusty.

- Use shoe trees to help them keep their shape, especially when packed away for the season. For tall boots, you can roll up old magazines and stick them in the shafts to help them stay upright.

- Polish or buff leather shoes at least once a season, and periodically brush suede shoes to remove surface dirt and preserve the nap.

- Try not to wear the same shoes two days in a row; alternating footwear not only gives your feet a break (preventing blisters, for example) but also gives your shoes a break from outdoor elements, wear and tear, and your sweat.

- If your shoes get wet, stuff them with newspaper to soak up the moisture. (No newspaper on hand to repurpose? Use a towel instead.)

- Check the soles regularly. If you know you'll be walking quite a bit in leather or synthetic-soled shoes, have a cobbler put taps on the toe and heel to keep them newer for longer. If you're staring at soles that are already worn down (keep a vigilant eye on the heels, especially), bring them to the cobbler ASAP—they may need to be entirely replaced to save the shoes.

DONATE SHOES TO BE REDISTRIBUTED OR RECYCLED.

Aside from donating shoes to your favorite local charity, you can also send them to companies and organizations that recycle and redistribute shoes to others in need. Here are a few national programs:

- Ship your shoes to Soles4Souls. They accept new and gently worn athletic shoes, running shoes, dress shoes, sandals, pumps, heels, work boots, cleats, dance shoes, and flip-flops— and they'll either give them directly to disaster victims in need of shoes or to microenterprises in Haiti, Central America, and parts of Africa to recondition and sell locally.

- Drop off your old, worn-out gym shoes (of any brand) at a participating Nike store, and they'll recycle the materials through their Reuse-a-Shoe program. The resulting material, called Nike Grind, is used to create new footwear, apparel, and field, track, and court surfaces.

- Got prom-worthy pumps, sandals, or flats? Drop them off at a local chapter of Becca's Closet, a nonprofit that provides teen girls with formal dresses, shoes, and accessories to wear to their proms.

BUY GENDER-NEUTRAL KIDS' CLOTHING.

Got a little one—or more? Then you know how quickly they grow, sizing out of shoes and clothing so fast that the items are practically still new by the time they've outgrown them. Choosing gender-neutral clothing ensures that you'll be able to use the items with your next child or pass them along to friends or family members, no matter what gender their offspring might be. Yes, boys can wear pink and girls can wear truck T-shirts, but the more universal the colors, styles, and designs of their clothes, the easier it will be to hand them off to a new kid again, and again, and again.

Wash your jeans less often.

There's a lot of talk about how environmentally unfriendly denim is—from the cotton used to make it (which requires large amounts of water, land, and other natural resources, and relies heavily on chemicals for growth and disease prevention) to the sometimes synthetic indigo dyes (whose runoff from factories pollutes area rivers[6]) and harsh chemicals used to produce custom rinses and finishes. But in terms of carbon dioxide emissions over the lifetime of a pair of jeans, 18.6 kg comes from washing them; that's more than the total CO_2 emissions created from growing the cotton; cutting, sewing, and finishing the denim; and transporting it to the retail outlet, according to *Blue Jeans: Environmental Aspects and Opportunities to Reduce the Environmental Impact*, a report commissioned by the International Solid Waste Association. While you don't have to follow as extreme a denim-care regimen as Levi's CEO Chip Bergh, who went on record saying he doesn't wash his denim in the washing machine, period, you could take a cue from the brand's official stance, which is that denim should be washed about once a month (unless you happen to get a stain on your pair, of course).[7] That advice is meant to prolong the life and look of your denim—and the environmental savings are an added benefit.

Quit the dry cleaner.

You drop off your clothes in one big jumble in your reusable laundry sack, and they come back on metal hangers, individually packaged—sometimes with paper liners—in plastic bags. Some cleaners will let you bring back your hangers and even provide your own garment bag, which can help bring a trip to the dry cleaner's down toward zero waste—but don't forget about the chemical solvents used to clean the clothes. Traditionally, cleaners use perchloroethylene ("perc"), a chemical that's considered by the state of California to be known to cause cancer (bladder, esophageal, stomach, intestinal, and pancreatic) and reproductive toxicity. It also impacts the environment: according to a fact sheet put out by SF Environment, a department of the city and county of San Francisco,[8] perc has been shown to contaminate soil, water, and indoor and outdoor air. While some dry cleaners have switched to ostensibly less damaging solvents (GreenEarth®, which contains decamethylcyclopentasiloxane, or D5; or hydrocarbons such as DF-2000, EcoSolv, Shell Sol, and Pure Dry), no solution is completely without environmental impact. The fact sheet reports that D5 has been found in human and fish tissue, and petroleum-based hydrocarbon solvents emit smog and contribute to global warming.

As an alternative, you can hand-wash wool, silk, cotton, linen, and most polyester fabrics at home. Just don't confuse hand-washing with "machine washing on delicate cycle." If you've ever put a beloved wool sweater in the machine only to have it come out shrunk to doll size, you won't be making that mistake twice. Instead, fill a basin (sink, tub, or large bucket) with cool water and a bit of gentle wool-wash detergent or even baby shampoo. Then gently soak and swirl your items one at a time. Give each one a rinse, and then blot water from them using a towel and shape and lay flat to dry on another towel or drying rack—or both.

Hang a clothesline.

The typical clothes dryer can consume as much energy as a new refrigerator, dishwasher, and clothes washer combined,[9] according to the NRDC. While newer, more energy-efficient models might use less energy, the majority of homes in the United States have machines that are older than five years[10]—and 30 percent are older than ten years. The NRDC estimates that if we all switched to the most energy-efficient models available, it would prevent approximately sixteen million tons of carbon dioxide emissions annually,[11] which is equal to the pollution from three coal-fired power plants. But for an (almost) zero-waste approach, don't send your inefficient dryer to the outdated electronics graveyard—instead, hang a clothesline. Whether you hang it in your bathroom, laundry room, or your yard, it's an inexpensive and zero-waste way to dry your clothing. Additionally, it might just extend the life of your garments. In a study conducted by the American Chemical Society,[12] researchers found that high-temperature drying reduced the strength of cotton fabric by 25 percent or more. Spandex and other elastic fibers are also susceptible to heat damage. Drying your clothes on a line, rack, or hanger can preserve their shape; prevent them from rubbing against other clothes in the dryer, which can make the fabric look worn; and reduce your carbon footprint. Plus, if you air-dry clothes indoors during the winter months, you're naturally humidifying the dry air, at no cost to you or the planet.

SWADDLE YOUR BABY IN CLOTH DIAPERS, NOT DISPOSABLE.

Even the littlest members of the household can live (almost) zero-waste, starting with their diapers. While researchers have found that making disposable diapers and washing reusable ones takes roughly the same amount of energy,[13] cloth diapers have the advantage when it comes to landfill disposal. According to recent estimates, 4.3 million tons of diapers ended up in landfills in the United States over the course of one year (and no, that doesn't include the human waste that's thrown out with them).[14] Organic cloth diapers can be made from cotton, hemp, or bamboo, and while none of these fibers is impact-free when it comes to the environment, they're closer to zero-waste than traditional disposable diapers, which typically contain wood pulp; a super absorbent polymer (SAP) of either petroleum-derived sodium polyacrylate or polyacrylate absorbents; polyethylene and polyester sheets; elastic; and polypropylene tape.[15]

SIX

Live (Almost) Zero Waste in Your Community

When it comes to living (almost) zero waste in an effort to preserve our planet's resources and keep it from becoming one giant landfill, two things are true at the same time: we can each do our part as individuals to make a difference, and we should all work together to make a difference.

Every move you make to reduce the waste you generate helps bring down the overall amount. But when you come together with your friends, your neighbors, your coworkers—or all of them, all at once—you can accomplish bigger change, and watch it spread from community to community.

Does that mean you have to steer every break-room conversation toward your new bar shampoo or the delicious bulk raw walnuts you discovered? Nope—nor do you have to volunteer details on your worm-rich compost heap at the next dinner party you attend. But it does mean that when a book-club pal asks you about your fantastic vintage jacket, you can let them know it wasn't just the retro style that caught your eye but also the fact that you were saving it from the landfill. That might even spark interest in a group trip to your favorite vintage clothing source, or lead to a seasonal clothing swap after the next book discussion.

If you're so inclined, you could also be an active voice against waste in your community—spearheading group cleanups and swaps, pushing for policy change, and spreading the message of reducing waste any way you can. What follows are ideas to bring the zero-waste mentality into your community in small ways, large ways, and any way that suits your personality, time, and interest.

CONTRIBUTE TO A COMMUNITY GARDEN.

Some community gardens grow food collectively for local food kitchens, while others give each member a spot to grow their own food and eat or share it as they see fit. Either way, growing more food close to home means less reliance on food flown or trucked in from out of town (fuel savings: check!), not to mention the opportunities for community composting—the larger the overall garden plot, the greater the need for soil-nourishing food scraps from everyone in town. A vibrant, flourishing community garden is also a great way to publicly promote the idea of growing your own food: often, these gardens are in public locations like empty lots, library lawns, or schoolyards, visible to all who pass by. When people stop to ask about your involvement, share a bit about what motivates you and how they can get started themselves.

Eight Benefits of Participating in a Community Garden[1]

- Access to fresh fruits, vegetables, and herbs.
- Socialization with fellow community members of all ages.

- Stress relief.
- Neighborhood beautification.
- Physical activity.
- More time spent in nature.
- Collaboration and cooperation.
- Healthier eating habits.

LEARN YOUR TOWN'S RECYCLING RULES.

We all think we know how to recycle, right? If only it were as simple as separating paper, plastic, and glass from your landfill-bound trash. Did you know that a grease-stained cardboard pizza box isn't recyclable? Or that a plastic supermarket bag needs to be recycled through special means, rather than mixed in with plastic water bottles and milk jugs? A quick search of your town or city's recycling rules will give you all the guidance you need to properly recycle. The details are important, because when a batch of recycling gets contaminated by a dirty item or one that simply doesn't belong (looking at you, flimsy plastic bag),[2] the entire load can be rejected—and sent straight to the landfill.

PICK UP AFTER OTHERS.

One way to work to change other people's behavior is to lead by example. When you spot a discarded water bottle on the ground, pick it up and take it to the nearest recycling bin. Notice a stray sandwich wrapper on the beach? Bring it to the trash bin. Yes, you're going out of your way to save the planet from being overrun by other people's waste, but you're also modeling good behavior for everyone in sight—and hopefully your sense of responsibility will be catching. There are thousands of people around the world picking up random litter every day, and even documenting it with photos and tags on sites like Litterati.org. Use that sense of community to motivate and challenge you, while inspiring others to follow in your footsteps.

ORGANIZE A LARGER COMMUNITY CLEANUP.

Once you identify a spot in town that's strewn with refuse—the local ball field, public park, or even the corner lot at the end of your street—head to your town council or city hall and find out how to organize a community cleanup. If you get the town behind it, you might be able to publicize your cleanup on the municipal Facebook page, official website, or even through the schools. Here's a list of other things to consider when planning:

- Date and time. (Plus rain date and time.)
- How will trash and recycling be collected—and where will it go at the end of the day?
- Can all ages get involved?

- Does the town require permits?
- How will you spread the word?
- Will you provide (recycled-material) trash bags or ask individuals to bring their own?

START A DONATION DRIVE.

Inspiration might come from your own excess (too many coats! unused toiletries!) or from a need in your community. Either way, if you're rounding up your own items to donate, go the extra step and ask community members to do the same. You can make your drive as large or small as you want: include only a close circle of friends or the whole darn town. Just make sure to reach out to the charity first in order to see what sort of guidelines they have for large-scale donations. Dress for Success, for example, offers a "clothing drive kit" you can access on their website, with tips on remembering to designate storage space for items, sample language for recruiting donors, and more.

USE THE LIBRARY.

Visiting your local library can give you access to so much more than what's contained in the building itself. Libraries in the same counties or consortiums often share resources, increasing your options and allowing you to borrow content from a vast network across the region.

What's more, your library likely also has a digital collection, meaning you can access an e-library filled with digital books, audiobooks, and electronic-hold options that alert you when your chosen book is ready for loan. Beyond books, your library might also offer a digital entertainment lending app that will give you access to movies, television series, and more. With fewer hard-copy forms of entertainment coming into your home, you'll have less to get rid of once your bookshelves are packed or the technology has changed. (Just ask anyone who invested in a huge CD collection in the 1990s.)

ASK YOUR CITY ABOUT CURBSIDE ORGANIC PICKUP.

As more of these programs pop up in cities around the country, more food waste and soiled paper (those greasy pizza boxes included) are being composted instead of sent to the landfill to create the greenhouse gas methane as it decomposes. The specifics vary from city to city—in some locations participation is mandatory, and in other areas households must sign up to join[3]—but the gist is the same: you collect your food waste and certain soiled paper products and then put them out at the curb for pickup along with recyclable materials.

START A LITTLE FREE LIBRARY.

Got books to spare? Share them with the community—

and encourage others to do the same—by setting up a Little Free Library in your town. The idea is simple: you store and display books for borrowing in a wooden structure that's easily accessible to the public, so that they can browse, borrow, donate, and return books at their leisure. Details, tips, and even pre-built models can be found on LittleFreeLibrary.org—along with an interactive map that lets you find the closest LFL to you.

Donate Unwanted Materials to Animal Shelters.

All those furry four-legs waiting to be adopted need supplies to keep them fed, warm, and comfortable—and your discarded fleece blankets, towels, and even socks (which can be used as newborn kitten hats or stuffed with uncooked rice to make bed warmers) might do the trick for a local shelter. Many shelters list acceptable items for donation on their websites, but if you don't see the information on yours, call them directly. Some supplies on the Humane Society's list of donation items include newspaper, long-shredded office paper, and clean plastic shopping bags.

Offer to Host a Zero-Waste Program at the Library.

Library directors are always looking for interesting programs to present to the community, and if you have an area of expertise (even a fledgling one!), consider sharing your knowledge with others. If you've mastered composting, teach everyone else. If you now make all your own baby food from scratch, invite parents to a how-to event. A program on how to shop secondhand stores for gorgeous wardrobe finds would be popular, as would an image- and tip-driven account of your zero-waste home renovation. Share your passion, spread the word, and be part of a chain reaction of increasing responsibility to our environment and ourselves.

You're Already an (Almost) Zero-Waste Hero

Y ou read them—all 118 tips. Some you're probably doing already, some you might try today, and others tomorrow. But while this book is meant to be comprehensive in helping you reduce waste across all parts of your life, it's by no means complete. Every day, people are finding new and innovative ways to consume more consciously, reuse more creatively, and lend and borrow things we might not have done a generation—or even a decade!—ago. (Car sharing. Amazing.)

Take these ideas and make them your own, then tell curious friends, family, and strangers exactly how they can make these changes in their own lives. And don't forget the *why*—the more we share the statistics and facts about waste and how it's impacting our planet, the more we'll all recognize the importance of making changes for the better.

It's possible that in a year's time, all the waste you've generated over the year will fit neatly into one Mason jar. (You've read the blogs—you know it can happen.) But it's also possible that you won't be able to quantify the ways you've improved your eco-footprint. Don't sweat it; just feel good knowing that your recycling bin isn't as full because you're buying and using less packaging. Know that you haven't tossed leftovers in months, and that you keep a stainless steel fork and knife at your desk for lunch. Know that those shoes you couldn't walk half a block in have been donated to someone who might find them more comfortable. Let your successes inspire you to take on more zero-waste habits and behaviors. It all matters. It all makes a difference.

Everything you do is saving the planet and everyone on it. Keep up the great work.

(And if you feel like hashtagging, I'd love to see what you're up to—and to try your tips and strategies! #almostzerowaste)

Acknowledgments

Thanks to all the hard-core zero wasters who inspire the rest of us. Thanks to everyone who picked up this book with the intention of doing a little more to reduce their waste than they were doing yesterday. Thanks to Darby Hoover of the Natural Resources Defense Council, who answered all my crazy hypotheticals and gave us all permission to do the best we can without feeling guilty about what we aren't doing. Thanks to my husband, who blurted out zero-waste ideas at the dinner table, and to my friends and family, who shared their best tips. Thanks to my editor, Lauren Hummel, who pushed me to come up with the best, most actionable yet realistic ways to live almost zero waste, and also to Theresa DiMasi, whose confidence propelled me through this book from start to finish.

And a huge thanks to our planet. Having written this book, I can never again take anything we have here on Earth for granted. I clean up other people's litter at the beach, I fish unwashed plastics out of the recycling can to rinse them out, and I seek out the best places to donate unwanted clothing and household items so that they will truly be put to use. (And I also keep an empty Mason jar on my office shelf as a reminder that there's always a little more I can do.)

Notes

Introduction

1. "Global Waste to Grow by 70 Percent by 2050 Unless Urgent Action Is Taken: World Bank Report," press release, September 20, 2018, https://www.worldbank.org/en/news/press -release/2018/09/20/global-waste-to-grow-by-70 -percent-by-2050-unless-urgent-action-is-taken -world-bank-report.
2. Carly Cassella, "Nearly 25% of the World's Population Faces a Water Crisis, And We Can't Ignore It," August 7, 2019, https://www.sciencealert .com/17-countries-are-facing-extreme-water-stress -and-they-hold-a-quarter-of-the-world-s-population.
3. Shannyn Snyder, "Water Scarcity—The US Connection," https://thewaterproject.org/water -scarcity/water_scarcity_in_us.

Chapter One:
Eat and Cook (Almost) Zero Waste

1. Dana Gunders, "Wasted: How America Is Losing up to 40 Percent of Its Food from Farm to Fork to Landfill," NRDC Issue Paper, August 2012, https:// www.nrdc.org/sites/default/files/wasted-food-IP.pdf.
2. Eco-Cycle, "Be Straw Free Campaign: Frequently Asked Questions," http://www.ecocycle.org /bestrawfree/faqs.

3. For a Strawless Ocean, "Understanding Plastic Pollution," https://www.strawlessocean.org/faq.

4. American Society of Agronomy, "Landfill Cover Soil Methane Oxidation Underestimated," *ScienceDaily*, May 1, 2009, https://www.sciencedaily.com /releases/2009/04/090427121637.htm.

5. Mandy Oaklander, "92% of Restaurant Meals Have Too Many Calories: Study," *Time*, January 20, 2016, https://time.com/4187120/restaurant-meals -fast-food-calories/.

6. Lisa Jennings, "What Restaurants Can Do to Reduce Food Waste," Restaurant Hospitality, February 8, 2018, https://www.restaurant-hospitality.com /operations/what-restaurants-can-do-reduce-food -waste.

7. Taylor Orci, "Are Tea Bags Turning Us into Plastic?" *Atlantic*, April 8, 2013, https://www .theatlantic.com/health/archive/2013/04/are-tea-bags -turning-us-into-plastic/274482/.

8. Valentina Bisinella, Paola Federica Albizzati, Thomas Fruergaard Astrup, and Anders Damgaard, eds., "Life Cycle Assessment of Grocery Carrier Bags," Danish Environmental Protection Agency, February 2018, https://www2.mst.dk/Udgiv /publications/2018/02/978-87-93614-73-4.pdf.

9. Zoë Schlanger, "Your Cotton Tote Is Pretty Much the Worst Replacement for a Plastic Bag," Quartz, April 1, 2019, https://qz.com/1585027/when-it -comes-to-climate-change-cotton-totes-might-be -worse-than-plastic/.

10. Charles P. Gerba, David Williams, and Ryan G. Sinclair, "Assessment of the Potential for Cross Contamination of Food Products by Reusable Shopping Bags," Loma Linda University School of Public Health, October 17, 2013, https:// publichealth.llu.edu/about/blog/dr-ryan-sinclair -reusable-shopping-bag-study.

11. Catherine Boeckmann, "10 Easy Vegetables to Grow from Seed," *Old Farmer's Almanac*, January 18, 2019, https://www.almanac.com/content/10-easy -vegetables-grow-seed.

12. "Meatless Monday History," Monday Campaigns, https://www.meatlessmonday.com /about-us/history/.

13. J. Poore and T. Nemecek, "Reducing Food's Environmental Impacts through Producers and Consumers," *Science* 360, no. 6392 (June 1, 2018): 987–92, https://science.sciencemag.org /content/360/6392/987.

14. "Composting at Home," Environmental Protection Agency, https://www.epa.gov/recycle /composting-home.

15. Pamela M. Geisel and Donna C. Seaver, "Composting Is Good for Your Garden and the Environment," University of California Division of Agriculture and Natural Resources, https:// anrcatalog.ucanr.edu/pdf/8367.pdf.

16. "Confused by Date Labels on Packaged Foods?" Food & Drug Administration, https://www.fda.gov /consumers/consumer-updates/confused-date-labels -packaged-foods.

Chapter Two:
Create an (Almost) Zero-Waste Home

1. "National Overview: Facts and Figures on Materials, Wastes, and Recycling," Environmental Protection Agency, https://www.epa.gov/facts-and -figures-about-materials-waste-and-recycling /national-overview-facts-and-figures-materials.

2. "Sustainable Agriculture: Cotton: Overview," World Wildlife Fund, https://www.worldwildlife.org /industries/cotton.

3. "State Rainwater Harvesting Laws and Legislation," National Conference of State Legislatures, February

2, 2018, http://www.ncsl.org/research/environment
-and-natural-resources/rainwater-harvesting.aspx.
4. M. Haberland, M. Bakacs, and S. Yergeau, "An
Investigation of the Water Quality of Rainwater
Harvesting Systems," *Journal of the NACAA* 6, no.
1 (May 2013), https://www.nacaa.com/journal/index
.php?jid=205.
5. "Advancing Sustainable Materials Management:
2015 Fact Sheet," Environmental Protection Agency,
https://www.epa.gov/sites/production/files/2018-07
/documents/2015_smm_msw_factsheet_07242018
_fnl_508_002.pdf.
6. "Pledge to 'Wipe Right': Use Recycled Toilet Paper,"
NRDC, https://act.nrdc.org/sign/recycled-tp
-pledge-190826.
7. "About Amazon Certified Frustration-Free
Packaging," Amazon.com, https://www
.amazon.com/gp/help/customer/display
.html?nodeId=201910210.
8. "Lighting Choices to Save You Money," US
Department of Energy, https://www.energy.gov
/energysaver/save-electricity-and-fuel/lighting
-choices-save-you-money.
9. Rachel Swalin, "Should You Leave the TV or Radio
on for Your Pets?" Health.com, March 13, 2015,
https://www.health.com/pets/should-you-leave
-the-radio-on-for-your-pets.
10. "Thermostats," US Department of Energy, https://
www.energy.gov/energysaver/thermostats.
11. "Smart Thermostats," EnergyStar.gov, https://www
.energystar.gov/products/heating_cooling
/programmable_thermostats/proper_use_guidelines.
12. Amanda Nicholson, "Washington Enacts Law
Creating New Paint Recycling Program," Product
Stewardship Institute, May 9, 2019, https://www
.productstewardship.us/news/450750/Washington

-Enacts-Law-Creating-New-Paint-Recycling
-Program.htm.

13. "Donate," Habitat for Humanity ReStore, https://
pdxrestore.org/donate.

14. "Statistics of the Year 2018: Winners Announced,"
Royal Statistical Society, https://www
.statslife.org.uk/news/4026-statistics-of-the
-year-2018-winners-announced.

15. "Composting Dog Waste," US Department of
Agriculture, https://www.nrcs.usda.gov/Internet/FSE
_DOCUMENTS/nrcs142p2_035763.pdf.

16. "Grow a Healthy, No-Waste Lawn and Garden,"
Minnesota Pollution Control Agency, https://www
.pca.state.mn.us/living-green/grow-healthy-no-waste
-lawn-and-garden.

17. Mary Talbot, "More Sustainable (and Beautiful)
Alternatives to a Grass Lawn," Natural Resources
Defense Council, September 30, 2016, https://www
.nrdc.org/stories/more-sustainable-and-beautiful
-alternatives-grass-lawn.

18. Linda Ly, "Eco-Friendly Alternatives to a Grassy
Lawn," Gilmour.com, https://gilmour.com/grass
-alternatives-backyard-lawn.

19. "The Secret Life of a Smart Phone," Environmental
Protection Agency, https://www.epa.gov/sites
/production/files/2015-06/documents/smart_phone
_infographic_v4.pdf.

20. Art Swift, "Americans Split on How Often They
Upgrade Their Smartphones," Gallup.com, https://
news.gallup.com/poll/184043/americans-split-often
-upgrade-smartphones.aspx.

21. "Durable Goods: Product-Specific Data," Furniture
and Furnishings entry, Environmental Protection
Agency, https://www.epa.gov/facts-and
-figures-about-materials-waste-and-recycling/durable
-goods-product-specific-data#main-content.

Chapter Three:
Maintain (Almost) Zero-Waste Personal Care

1. M. Shahbandeh, "Cosmetics Industry in the U.S.— Statistics & Facts," Statista, October 24, 2019, https://www.statista.com/topics/1008/cosmetics -industry.

2. "The Environmental Consumer's Handbook," Environmental Protection Agency, 1990, https:// nepis.epa.gov/Exe/ZyPDF.cgi/2000URC7. PDF?Dockey=2000URC7.PDF.

3. Hair color information page, Aveda.com, https:// www.aveda.com/hair-color.

4. "Henna Hair Dyes," Lush.com, https://www .lushusa.com/hair/henna-hair-dyes/.

5. "What Are Microbeads?" Beat the Microbead, Plastic Soup Foundation, https://www .beatthemicrobead.org/.

6. Alejandra Borunda, "How Your Toothbrush Became a Part of the Plastic Crisis," *National Geographic*, June 14, 2019, https://www.nationalgeographic .com/environment/2019/06/story-of-plastic -toothbrushes/.

7. Thomas J. Salinas, DDS, "Is It More Effective to Floss Teeth with a Water Pick or Standard Dental Floss?" Mayo Clinic, April 20, 2018, https://www .mayoclinic.org/healthy-lifestyle/adult-health/expert -answers/dental-floss/faq-20058112.

8. "What Not to Flush," Ryerson Today, April 5, 2019, https://www.ryerson.ca/news-events /news/2019/04/what-not-to-flush/.

9. Michael Veronin, "Packaging and Labeling of Pharmaceutical Products Obtained from the Internet," *Journal of Medical Internet Research* 13, no. 1 (January–March 2011): e22, https://www.ncbi .nlm.nih.gov/pmc/articles/PMC3221344/.

10. "How Often Should You Wash Your (Germ Magnet of a) Bath Towel?" Health Essentials, Cleveland

Clinic, January 16, 2019, https://health
.clevelandclinic.org/how-often-should-you-wash
-your-germ-magnet-of-a-bath-towel/.

11. "30+ Natural Brands with Zero Waste or
Sustainable Packaging," *Organically Becca* (blog),
April 24, 2018, https://organicallybecca.com/zero
-waste-sustainable-packaging/.

12. Roddy Scheer and Doug Moss, "Scent of Danger:
Are There Toxic Ingredients in Perfumes and
Colognes?" *Scientific American*, September 29,
2012, https://www.scientificamerican.com/article
/toxic-perfumes-and-colognes/.

13. Carina Hsieh and Hannah Smothers, "The 14 Best
Organic Tampon Brands, Because Your Vagina
Deserves It," *Cosmopolitan*, December 6, 2019,
https://www.cosmopolitan.com/sex-love/a13144732
/best-organic-tampons/.

14. "PVC Disposal and Recycling," SFGate, https://
homeguides.sfgate.com/pvc-disposal-recycling
-79234.html.

Chapter Four:
Travel Near and Far with (Almost) Zero Waste

1. "Inventory of U.S. Greenhouse Gas Emissions and
Sinks," Environmental Protection Agency, https://
www.epa.gov/ghgemissions/inventory-us-greenhouse
-gas-emissions-and-sinks.

2. "Transit's Role in Environmental Sustainability,"
Federal Transit Administration, May 9, 2016,
https://www.transit.dot.gov/regulations-and
-guidance/environmental-programs/transit
-environmental-sustainability/transit-role.

3. Laura Bliss, "Carpooling Is Totally Coming Back
This Time, We Swear," CityLab, September 15,
2017, https://www.citylab.com/transportation
/2017/09/is-carpooling-making-a-
comeback/539979/.

4. "Electric Vehicle Benefits and Considerations," US Department of Energy, https://afdc.energy.gov/fuels/electricity_benefits.html.

5. "Electric Vehicles: Tax Credits and Other Incentives," US Department of Energy, https://www.energy.gov/eere/electricvehicles/electric-vehicles-tax-credits-and-other-incentives.

6. "Electric Vehicles and Solar Incentives," Tesla, https://www.tesla.com/support/incentives.

7. "Idling Reduction for Personal Vehicles," US Department of Energy, https://afdc.energy.gov/files/u/publication/idling_personal_vehicles.pdf.

8. Riley Hutchings and Kim Tyrrell, "Putting the Brakes on Idling Vehicles," National Conference of State Legislatures, September 11, 2018, http://www.ncsl.org/research/environment-and-natural-resources/putting-the-brakes-on-idling-vehicles.aspx.

9. "Keeping Your Vehicle in Shape," US Department of Energy, https://www.fueleconomy.gov/feg/maintain.jsp.

10. "Regulations for Greenhouse Gas Emissions from Aircraft," Environmental Protection Agency, https://www.epa.gov/regulations-emissions-vehicles-and-engines/regulations-greenhouse-gas-emissions-aircraft.

11. Yoon Jung, "Fuel Consumption and Emissions from Airport Taxi Operations," NASA Ames Research Center, https://flight.nasa.gov/pdf/18_jung_green_aviation_summit.pdf.

12. Heinrich Bofinger and Jon Strand, "Calculating the Carbon Footprint from Different Classes of Air Travel," World Bank Development Research Group, http://documents.worldbank.org/curated/en/141851468168853188/pdf/WPS6471.pdf.

13. "Carbon Offsetting and Reduction Scheme for International Aviation (CORSIA)," International

Civil Aviation Organization, United Nations, https://www.icao.int/environmental-protection/CORSIA/Pages/default.aspx.

14. Jack Stewart, "Stop Worrying about Buying Carbon Offsets for Your Flights," *Wired*, November 20, 2018, https://www.wired.com/story/airline-emissions-carbon-offsets-travel/.

15. A. Konieczna, A. Rutkowska, and D. Rachoń, "Health Risk of Exposure to Bisphenol A (BPA)," *Roczniki Panstwowego Zakladu Higieny* 66, no. 1 (2015): 5–11, https://www.ncbi.nlm.nih.gov/pubmed/25813067.

16. Jeff Sossamon, "Thermal Paper Cash Register Receipts Account for High Bisphenol A (BPA) Levels in Humans, MU Study Finds," MU News Bureau, October 22, 2014, https://munewsarchives.missouri.edu/news-releases/2014/1022-thermal-paper-cash-register-receipts-account-for-high-bisphenol-a-bpa-levels-in-humans-mu-study-finds/.

17. Joseph P. Fuhr and Stephen Pociask, "Broadband and Telecommuting: Helping the US Environment and the Economy," *Low Carbon Economy* 2 (2011): 41–47, https://file.scirp.org/pdf/LCE20110100004_53025817.pdf.

Chapter Five:
Build an (Almost) Zero-Waste Wardrobe

1. "Textiles: Material-Specific Data," Environmental Protection Agency, https://www.epa.gov/facts-and-figures-about-materials-waste-and-recycling/textiles-material-specific-data.

2. Luz Claudio, "Waste Couture: Environmental Impact of the Clothing Industry," *Environmental Health Perspectives* 115, no. 9 (September 1, 2007), https://ehp.niehs.nih.gov/doi/10.1289/ehp.115-a449.

3. Kate Carter, "Pandering to the Green Consumer," *Guardian*, August 12, 2008, https://www

.theguardian.com/lifeandstyle/2008/aug/13/bamboo
.fabric.

4. Christina Sewell, "From Apples to Kombucha Tea: See the Ingenious Way Designers are Making Vegan Leather," PETA, https://www.peta.org/living /personal-care-fashion/vegan-leather-chic-sustainable -and-fruity/.

5. Susanne Maria Krauß, "East Africa Pushes Secondhand Clothing Ban," DW.com, February 26, 2018, https://www.dw.com/en/east-africa-pushes -second-hand-clothing-ban/a-42747222.

6. Haisam Hussein, "Your Jeans Are Ruining the Earth," *Vice*, September 25, 2017, https://www.vice .com/en_us/article/kzzpjm/your-jeans-are-ruining-the -earth-v24n7.

7. Olivia Petter, "How Often Should You Wash Your Jeans?" *Independent*, March 29, 2019, https://www.independent.co.uk/life-style/fashion /jeans-wash-how-often-many-times-levis -boss-a8845411.html.

8. "Dry Cleaning: How to Green Your Cleaning," SF Environment, https://sfenvironment.org/sites /default/files/fliers/files/sfe_th_dry_cleaning_how_to _green_your_cleaning.pdf.pdf.

9. Amanda MacMillan, "Easy Ways to Save Energy at Home," Natural Resources Defense Council, https:// www.nrdc.org/stories/easy-ways-save-energy-home.

10. Ibid.

11. "A Call to Action for More Efficient Clothes Dryers: US Consumers Missing Out on $4 Billion in Annual Savings," NRDC Issue Brief, June 2014, https:// www.nrdc.org/sites/default/files/efficient -clothes-dryers-IB.pdf.

12. "Cotton Fabrics Damaged by High Dryer Temperatures," *ScienceDaily*, August 31, 1999, https://www.sciencedaily.com/releases/1999 /08/990831080157.htm.

13. "An Updated Lifecycle Assessment for Disposable and Reusable Nappies," UK Environment Agency, https://www.gov.uk/government/publications /an-updated-lifecycle-assessment-for-disposable-and -reusable-nappies.

14. "Nondurable Goods: Product-Specific Data: Disposable Diapers," Environmental Protection Agency, https://www.epa.gov/facts-and-figures-about -materials-waste-and-recycling/nondurable-goods -product-specific-data#main-content.

15. Juliet Spurrier, MD, "What Is Inside Those Disposable Diapers?" BabyGearLab, May 24, 2018, https://www.babygearlab.com/expert-advice/what-is -inside-those-disposable-diapers.

Chapter Six:
Live (Almost) Zero Waste in Your Community

1. Dr. Lucy Bradley, "Research Regarding the Benefits of Community Gardens," North Carolina State University Extension, https://nccommunitygardens .ces.ncsu.edu/nccommunitygardens-research/.

2. David Henslovitz, Ava Landgraf, Alex Robinson, Karishma Satapathy, and Nathan Vellayan, "Recycling Bin Contamination," Planet Blue, University of Michigan, http://sustainability.umich .edu/environ211/recycling-bin-contamination.

3. Virginia Streeter and Brenda Platt, "Residential Food Waste Collection Access in the US," *BioCycle* 58, no. 11 (December 2017): 20, https://www .biocycle.net/2017/12/06/residential-food-waste -collection-access-u-s/.

Index

Vietnam Veterans of America, 106
vinyl plank flooring, 42
VOCs (volatile organic compounds), 42, 102

W

walking, 86
wardrobe, 101–18 (*see also* shoes)
  capsule, 103–4
  clotheslines, 116–17
  clothing swaps, 107–9, 125
  donation of, 105–6, 128
  dry cleaning, 115
  gender-neutral, 113
  hand-washing, 115–16
  jeans, washing, 114
  secondhand, 104, 105–6, 131
  sewing or tailoring, 106–7
  sustainable brands, 109–10
  synthetic fabrics, 102
  vegan leather, 104–5
washcloths, 73

washing dishes, 49
"Waste Couture: Environmental Impact of the Clothing Industry" (Claudio), 101–2
waste separation, 43
water scarcity, ix–x
weather reports, travel and, 93
weed killer, 33
wildflower lawns, 55
window replacement, 48
wood pulp, xvii, 33, 118
woodruff, 56
working from home, 96
workout clothes, 78
World Bank, 91

Y

yard waste, 19, 20
yoga mats, 79–81

Z

zinc, 35
zip-top bags, xiv, 9, 37

About the Author

Award-winning journalist **MELANIE MANNARINO** has written and created content for magazines including *Real Simple*, *Cosmopolitan*, and *Seventeen*, and has worked as deputy executive editor for *Redbook* and news editor for *Marie Claire*. The author of *The Best Gender-Neutral Baby Name Book* and *Epic Baby Names for Girls*, Melanie scours antique shops for vintage clothes, walks to mass transit, and repurposes leftovers like a pro. She lives in New Jersey with her husband, son, and two cats (who use biodegradable litter and love it).